1998

der's

Start-Up:

G_____ Snow**DATE DUE**g

2nd Edition / Completely Revised

By
Doug Werner & Jim Waide

Photography by Doug Werner
(except where indicated)

Start-Up Sports #2

Tracks Publishing
San Diego, California

Snowboarder's Start-Up:
A Beginner's Guide to Snowboarding
2nd Edition / Completely Revised

By Doug Werner & Jim Waide

Start-Up Sports / Tracks Publishing
140 Brightwood Avenue
Chula Vista, CA 91910
619-476-7125 Fax 619-476-8173

Publisher's Cataloging in Publication

Werner, Doug, 1950-
    Snowboarder's start-up : a beginner's guide to snowboarding / Doug Werner. – 1st ed.
    p. cm. – (Start-up sports ; #2)
    Includes bibliographical references and index.
    Preassigned LCCN: 98-61158.
    ISBN: 1-884654-11-8

1. Snowboarding.   I. Title.   II. Series.

GV857.S57W47 1998   796.9
                                     QBI98-1065

To Genie Wheeler

Acknowledgements:

Steve Leong
Kathleen Wheeler
Phyllis Carter
Jim Clinkscales
Mark Suchomel
Lynn's Photo
ColorType
Alison Thatcher
North Shores Printery
Douglas Waide
Transworld Snowboarding
Tammy Parsons
Ted Martin
Robin Niehaus
Craig McClain
Stu Kenson
Ann Werner
Gene Wheeler
Snow Summit
Snow Valley
John Stouffer
Lee Crane
Henry Hester
David Scribner
Marta Meler
Chris Bachman
Kevin Kinnear
Richard MacMahon
Richie Finegood
Bookcrafters

Preface:

Safe & Sane

McClain

Ask any rider to identify his greatest difficulty in learning how to snowboard and the reply will probably be, "My first day!" Every snowboarder I know has a sad tale to tell about his first time strapped to a slippery board. And I was no different. My first experience was a disaster. I got so trashed I thought I would never go back!

But the sport has come a long way since then. There is now a safe and sane way to learn how to board. The terrors and trials of learning are a myth. In these pages you'll find a step-by-step formula that will enable you to ride and enjoy yourself in a very short time.

So take notes and prepare to learn one of our planet's most thrilling pursuits.

Doug Werner

Contents

Preface: Safe & Sane   5
Introduction: Charge!   9

 1. Isn't Snowboarding Like ...   13
 2. Classroom   17
 3. Gear   27
 4. Carpet Riding   39
 5. Preparations   45
 6. On the Flats   53
 7. On a Small Hill   61
 8. Lifts   73
 9. Down the Mountain   79
10. Turns   91
    Carving   100
11. Interview: An Instructor's instructor   103
12. Safety   111
13. History   115

Glossary   127
Resources   133
Bibliography   137
Index   139

Why learn? Look at this rider's face!

Introduction:

Charge!

King of the Hill

Snowboarding has become one of the fastest growing sports in the world. The National Sporting Goods Association (NSGA) states that snowboarding grew 32.5% from 1995 to 1996 (that was *twice* as fast as soccer which showed the next largest rate of growth). According to American Sports Data (ASD) snowboarding grew *another 33%* from 1996 to 1997.

More and more guys like him want to snowboard. Period.

For years increasing numbers of young people have opted to learn snow-boarding over skiing, thus paving the way for its permanence on the hill. In 1996 the ratio of snow-boarders to skiers was 23%.

In 1997 it was 34%. For ages 6 through 11 it was 42%. For teenagers 46%. For ages 18–24 it was a whopping 77%.

But it isn't only the kids. The 25–34 age group grew 207% from 1996 to 1997. According to *Transworld Snowboarding Business* "this older crossover

9

demographic is where snowboarding continues to experience high growth."

Perhaps the most important news about this sport's place in the scheme of things isn't really about numbers. In 1997 snowboarding forever shed its outlaw colors and made its first appearance at the Olympic Games — a rather far-fetched idea not so very long ago.

It Only Feels Like Magic
Despite the popularity of snowboarding, available instructional material for the sport has lagged behind the curve. New and better methods of imparting basic  skills as they are taught by the leading instructors haven't been published. What you have are directives without the how or why, or worse, guides with conflicting explanations for the same thing. The result leaves the reader somewhat better informed about the sport in general, but confused about specific points of technique that really count.

How to control your downhill flight on a snowboard is not a mystery. There is a way to do it, and we will tell you how in this book. Gaining proficiency isn't magic although when you finally link those wonderful arcing turns it will certainly feel like it!

Role of This Book

This book is an introduction to the sport of snowboarding. Its purpose is to help the reader prepare for his or her first days of riding and to provide a simple reference. It's not intended to replace on-the-hill instruction. Nothing can replace good coaching! This book provides an overview, things to work on before you even show up at the snowboarding area and the basics you need to know in a simple, easy-to-review format.

Skiers versus Snowboarders

Of course the friction has faded. At one time, snowboarding was wildly new and a banner of reckless youth. Skiing was the established order of stuffy older folks (or something like that) and the two factions really, really annoyed each other.

These days snowboarding is much more a part of the mountain. First of all, snowboarders are quite a bit more skilled than they used to be. They're more in control and not the physical threat they were when they charged down the slopes without a clue. Second, the joys of snowboarding have become apparent to everyone. Even skiers like to snowboard and many cross over for good. Finally, the popularity of snowboarding demands that the ski industry pay attention to it. And it most certainly has. Snowboarding is very big business and getting bigger.

A Pioneer Story

Way back in 1979, a cadre of snowboarders managed to convince the powers at the Fairfield Snowbowl in Arizona to allow snowboarding. Understand that back then snowboarding was REALLY NEW and REALLY

DIFFERENT. And something to be suspicious of. Snowboarders could use the mountain only if they got on and off the lifts with some sort of skis. There was a question of control. The skis of choice were three-foot plastic models from the Goodwill. Go figure.

Anyway, within a month a snowboarder got into a fight with the ski patrol and the thread of tolerance was broken. Snowboarding was banned from the resort until 1986. The U.S. Forest Service labeled snowboards dangerous "non-directional devices."

That's a sinister citation. The uninitiated must have imagined that snowboarders just tore off down the slope on "devices" that could not be steered. Visions of wild youth careening into trees, skiers, lift lines and the disco must have exploded in some bureaucrat's head.

So the sport went underground in Arizona. Or to be more precise — it went nocturnal. Guerrilla snowboarders befriended the snocat drivers who groomed the trails at night. Riders got lifts up the mountain, and in the glare of the snocat headlights, boarded back down.

Understand that snocats are very big pieces of equipment. Sort of like the machines at the beginning of the Terminator movie. They've got these scary tank treads that can squish anything in their path. Snowboarding in front of one of these monsters must have been, well, thrilling. And a real incentive to get good. As in never, ever falling.

Chapter One:

Isn't Snowboarding Like ...

Surfing?

I can understand why some people call snowboarding snow surfing. At a glance, you see a surfer-type guy or

gal standing surfer-like on a board, whizzing and twirling and jumping through the snow. Like a surfer whizzes and twirls and jumps (well, sometimes) on the face of a wave.

They certainly seem to belong to the same genre and there is a lot of crossover. In most surf shops within a half day's drive of the slopes you'll find snowboarding equipment for sale. There are contests that feature participants competing in both sports and they're held the same day (there's a long drive in between events). Both sports are naturalistic, individualistic, thrilling, young (thinking) and daring. Both require balance, flexibility, quick reflexes and a strong pair of legs.

But the physics of the sports are very different. A surfer rides a moving mass of water on a strapless (usually) surfboard. A snowboarder slides down a snow covered slope due to gravity and the planing surface of a board secured to his or her feet. Surfers intuitively turn off their back foot which is planted on the tail of a surfboard. Snowboarders on the other hand must learn to act counter-intuitively as they maneuver with their weight somewhat forward.

Skiing?
Skiing is not a dissimilar pursuit. Both skiing and snowboarding take advantage of the same physics at the same places. Both involve sliding, snow and mountains. Riders in both sports turn in and out of the fall line using the edges of their planing surfaces. The obvious difference is that skiers wear two slats and snowboarders wear one. So the two camps suffer different injuries, and depending whom you talk to, one sport is easier to learn than the other. Skiers also utilize bindings that release when you fall whereas snowboarders do not.

If you already know how to ski you probably have an advantage. Unlike blank slate novices, you have a feel for sliding on snow, edging on the slopes and soaking wet gloves.

Skateboarding?
Skateboarding has had a tremendous influence on snowboarding. So many of the acrobatics are inspired by the sport on wheels, especially those performed in the half-pipe. The ranks of snowboarders are replete with sidewalk shredders, including the guy who just may have started it all, Tom Sims. Of course, the stance is similar

and the act of skating downhill shares the gravity feed aspect of downhill snowboarding. That is, gravity provides the pull, hence the sliding on an inclined surface.

But skateboarders don't dig the edges of their boards into the asphalt to make a turn. They shift their weight and work with the special trucking devices that the wheels are attached to. Skateboards roll. They do not slide. The demands of edge control aren't involved in the physics of this sport.

So?

Snowboarding is somewhat like skiing and not so much like surfing or skateboarding. As a student it's best to approach the learning of snowboarding without the baggage of similarities. Snowboarding is definitely its own thing.

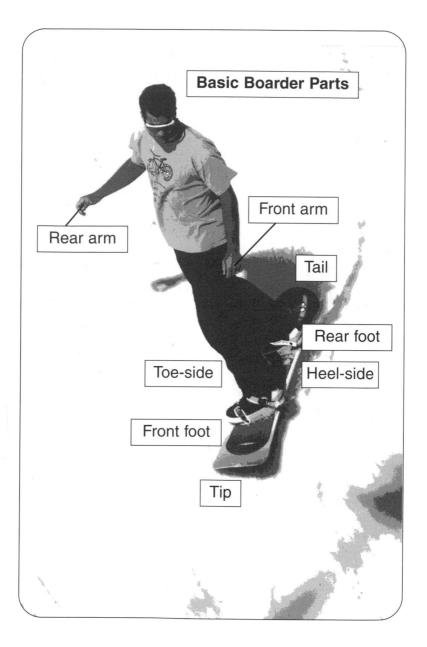

Basic Boarder Parts

Rear arm

Front arm

Tail

Rear foot

Toe-side

Heel-side

Front foot

Tip

Classroom

Anatomy of a Snowboarder on a Board

The novice snowboarder must decide which foot to strap in ahead of the other. Usually a right-hander will opt for left foot forward and a lefty the right foot forward. Try sliding in your stocking feet on the kitchen floor to see which foot you naturally place ahead of the other.

When you know which foot leads, you'll know your toe-side, your heel-side, your front shoulder and arm, and your rear shoulder and arm. The front of your snowboard is the tip and the back end is the tail. Your heel rests over the heel-side edge and your toes rest over the toe-side edge. There. Now you've got simple labels for everything.

Anatomy of a Snowboard

Besides the tip and tail, a snowboard has a deck on top

Labels: Tip, Deck, Bindings, Stomp Pad, Leash, Steel Edges, Tail

and a base on the bottom. Along the sides of the board are the steel edges as well as the board's sidecut. On the deck are bindings or places to secure each foot and in between is the stomp pad.

Snowboards have a number of characteristics but here are some important ones to remember for now.

Tip
The front of the board is curved up like a ski in order to slide over snow.

Tail
The tail may also be curved up in order to go backward (called fakie). The board you learn on should have some curve to the tail. Boards that have no tail lift are designed for advanced snowboarders who want to carve high speed turns or race.

Edges
The steel edges cut through and grip the snow during turns.

Sidecut
The sidecut enhances the effect of a turn. A turn occurs when the rider has weighted the board and flexed it so that the sidecut meets the snow.

Flex

Flex
Flex is the bendability of a snowboard and comes into play during a turn.

Camber

Camber refers to the bend built into a snowboard. Camber helps to distribute a rider's weight evenly over the board.

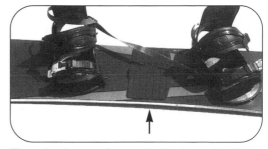

The shadow underneath the board indicates how the board naturally bends up in the middle without the rider's weight.

Stomp pad

The stomp pad is a secure, non-slippery place to rest your rear foot when not bound. Riders use it when exiting ski lifts or skating.

Leash

The leash attaches to your front leg. Although your bindings are designed not to release when you fall, you are always required to wear a leash. Runaway snowboards are very dangerous.

Sidecuts are the concave curves built into the sides of your snowboard. Sidecuts enhance the turning ability of a snowboard.

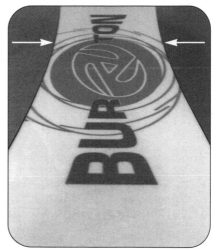

Some Physics

This can get really involved, so we'll keep it simple. You're going to learn how to slide down a hill on a snowboard. **Gravity** will pull you down on the plane of your snowboard. If you point yourself directly downhill you will naturally hurtle straight down the path of least resistance. This is called the **fall line**. If you let a ball roll down the face of the hill, it would take this path.

Since shooting the fall line at this point in your snowboarding career is like jumping out of an airplane without a parachute, it's important to learn how to **turn** back and forth across the fall line. This is how you control your speed and descent. Making a move to cross the fall line and slow down is called **traversing.**

Turning involves you and your body working in concert with the **edges** of your board. As stated earlier, the edges are the sides of the snowboard. Turns happen when one of the edges digs into the snow, creating resistance.

Here are the ingredients that make up a simple turn:

A combination of **rotation, pressuring** and **edging** will effect a direction change.

There is a science
to all this ...

But never mind
the physics. The
only formula you
need to know is:
    Up
+ Forward
+ Flatten
+ Wait
+ Rotate
+ Bend = Turn!
(You'll see.)

Rotation refers to the **full body rotation** a rider executes about halfway through a turn.

Pressuring is a combination of **unweighting** the snowboard immediately before a new turn and then **weighting** it as the turn begins and develops. Unweighting involves extending the legs and lifting up from the board. Weighting involves flexing the knees and sinking your weight down upon the board.

Edging occurs as a rider **rolls** the board from one edge to the other.

Developing and mastering these different skills and knowing when and how to apply them is key to controlling your downhill flight.

But This Ain't Natural!

Snowboarding (as well as skiing) are counter-intuitive pursuits. It is not natural to lean forward as gravity pulls you downhill. Instinct tells you to pull back. However, in order to successfully navigate your snowboard downhill, a majority of your weight must rest over the front foot. Weighting your rear foot will result in mishap. The board will simply shoot out from under you.

The desire to lean back is one of the major mental obstacles a rider must overcome. Everyone does it at first. But once you get the hang of it you'll *feel* the logic and embrace the "wrongness" of leaning forward in order to crank those turns.

Fear

The other mental obstacle is fear. Looking down even a beginner's slope for the first time is absolutely terrifying for some. You've got this clunky slat strapped to your feet, it's slippery as heck just standing in one spot for heaven's sake and you're being asked to slide off what appears to be the edge of the world! It's strange, uncomfortable and (oh yeah) unnatural. It's important to understand and to believe that there is a way to do this. You are not courting disaster.

Fear is so insidious. It'll make you anticipate mishap after mishap until that's all you'll have. Learn where you're comfy and have faith in your instructor and yourself. You can do this!

Physical Considerations

In the first edition I had this to say:

The kind of shape you're in will be evident in the first 45 minutes on the slopes. If you're in lousy shape, you'll die. If you're in OK shape, you'll die. If you're in good shape, you'll be exhausted. Don't be stupid. Be in shape. This snowboarding stuff is a lot work at first. And get a good night's sleep the night before.

Blunt and woefully short on particulars, but the point was made.

The reality of your first day involves a complex and trying physical challenge. High altitude cuts stamina and may even make you feel faint until you become more acclimated. Cold weather makes the body work double-time just standing still. Layers of clothing can be cumbersome. Coming to even the simplest terms (strapping in, walking around) with your snowboard is very awkward. Your initial movements on snow will be tense and erratic. Muscles will be asked to do things they have never done before. Falling down is tiresome. Being nervous is tiresome. Getting annoyed with a perceived lack of progress is tiresome.

All this adds up, and before you know it, you're really beat. So it's a good idea to prepare and plan a little for your snowboarding trip.

❑ Follow an exercise program for an ample length of time. Something aerobic that works legs and torso. Build stamina, lower body strength and flexibility. And stretch it out. You'll need it.

❏ Take a day or two to get used to the higher altitude before you go all out. Take it slow and expect to be slow for a while.

❏ Practice basic movements at home before you hit the slopes. This is good exercise for snowboarding and develops muscle memory. When you're finally up there, you'll be that much further along.

❏ Purchase or borrow lightweight, modern outdoor garb.

❏ Create reasonable goals for yourself. You want to measure your successes by how you feel and by how much fun you're having.

❏ Think about taking one step at a time in your learning and build a faith in the process. Look at your fears as simply small obstacles that will melt with time and experience. This is true: Behind the fear is the excitement and joy of downhill flight.

A Story About Desire
Make no bones about it. Snowboarding is a challenging sport to learn. You'll need patience, practice and concentration. But above all, you'll need desire. You gotta want it.

There was once a very determined young man who was seriously bitten by the snowboarding bug. However, he had a problem. No car. And he lived a long, long way from the snow.

It took some doing, but he managed to turn on a friend

of his who had wheels to the thrill and glory of his new found sport. Soon thereafter they headed out to the mountains. Unfortunately, the driver did not have a good day. Without instruction and little help from his friend, he pretty much ate snow all morning. After about three hours of that slamming sensation, he'd had enough. He was going home.

But the hero of our story was having none of that. He'd stay, by golly, shred all day and worry about getting home later! So he stayed and his ride left.

The ski area closed at 4:30 p.m. Our guy stuck out his thumb and began what turned out to be his own little Battan Death March. All this happened in early February of 1993 in Southern California. The time is important because that is when the biggest storms in ten years rattled through our state. It turned out to be a National Disaster with the works — flooding, torrential rains, mud slides, and lots and lots and lots of snow. Anyway, this manly man hitchhiked more than 200 miles through the howling weather because he wanted to snowboard a full day's worth. It took him twelve hours. He got home at 4:00 a.m. the next day.

There are all kinds of things we have to be dedicated to: making enough money, brushing our teeth, obeying traffic signs, changing the oil filter . . . But it's nice to be dedicated to something that essentially frees the spirit and is actually FUN! Although this particular episode is a tad extreme, it illustrates an important point or two about achieving a goal. You've got to want it and sometimes you have to sacrifice. Snowboarding is well worth the effort. Give it all you've got!

GQ!

Chapter Three:

Gear

Clothing
Yes, it's cold up there. And wet. Here's a checklist for proper clothing from head to toe.

Head
On cold days wear a cap or sock to cover dome and ears. A great deal of body heat can be lost through the head. If it's real cold, you'll want a mask.

Eyes
Wear sunglasses or goggles to protect the eyes from ultraviolet rays and the intense glare of snow and sun. Goggles also provide protection from the elements.

Upper Body
Wear layers of loose-fitting outdoor clothing. Layering provides versatility and climate control. Add layers to warm up against colder conditions and subtract layers to prevent overheating as the day grows warmer. Overheating causes perspiration (moisture), which robs the rider of heat through evaporation.

Tips for three layers:

Inner Layer
Start with a synthetic, moisture wicking body shirt that draws perspiration from the skin to the outer layers

where it can evaporate. *Do not wear cotton T-shirts.* As cotton absorbs moisture it loses its ability to insulate. Suitable synthetic materials include polypropylene, capilene, coolmax, ZeO2 or any similar nylon material that sheds water rather than absorbs it. If you sweat easily, bring an extra wicking layer to change into. Stay dry and you'll stay warm.

Middle Layers
This is your insulation layer. Wear layers of wool or suitable synthetic material to trap warm air.

Outer Layer
Wear a rugged, waterproof, breathable shell for protection from wind, rain and snow. Suitable shells are made from Gore-Tex or H2No, both which allow moisture to pass through, creating better temperature control.

Hands
Wear tough, waterproof mitts with wrist straps or gaiters to keep out snow. Consider wearing the wrist guards that skaters use. You will fall, and it's only natural to try to break your fall with an outstretched hand and arm. Suitable armor provides confidence as well as protection.

Lower Body
Like the upper body, wear synthetic, moisture wicking underwear. Over the long johns wear reinforced, waterproof and roomy snowboarding pants. Consider wearing padded pants for butt planting.

Feet
Wear wicking liner socks underneath wool or synthetic wool socks.

Outfitted: Robin rides a freestyle board with the tried and true freestyle (highback) bindings. His board measures just under chin-high. Note the soft boots and loose fit of his clothing.

Sunscreen
Your face will fry without it! You can't beat a water and sweat proof block of 30 SPF (sun protection factor).

Wasting Money, Losing Face
Talk about learning the hard way. The first two times I went snowboarding I forgot my goggles and nearly went blind from the glare. I didn't use sunscreen either. For three days after each trip I looked like I did a head dip into a pail of cranberry juice. I also got ripped for fifty bucks on a lift-lesson-rental package because I didn't shop the ski area twenty minutes down the road. It's easy for bad things to happen if you're unprepared. Poor planning can really cut into the fun and fun is what this is all about. Check into things and have a plan.

Boots, Boards & Bindings: In a Nutshell

Ideal
If you can, rent boots, board and bindings from a shop in your hometown the day before you go. This may be the least expensive way to rent, and it gives you time to comfortably acquaint yourself with the equipment. Much better to learn how to don all this new gear with a friendly salesperson in a cozy showroom than in a freezing parking lot. Or a crowded rental room at a ski area with a clerk who's too busy to care.

Renting from a local shop will give you the time to make all the adjustments you might need on your bindings and to ask questions. Your local shop will become your first source for gear, information and fellowship anyway. Might as well start there.

No Local Shop?
There should be shops surrounding the ski area you intend to visit. Check them out and call the ski areas. You might be able to get a package deal — lift tickets, gear and lessons. Then you won't have to hassle driving back and forth between places.

Boots
In general, there are soft boots and hard boots.

Soft boots are still the overwhelming favorite among snowboarders. Soft boots are comfortable and easy to walk around in. They are heavily padded and have thick rubber soles.

Hard boots and plate bindings on the left, soft boots and step-ins on the right.

There are soft boots designed to work with freestyle or highback bindings and soft boots designed to plug into step-in bindings. The latter have part of the binding apparatus built into the boot, which snaps onto a locking mechanism on the board and binding. Step-in boots have stiffeners built into them to provide neces-sary support and leverage.

You can wear hard snowboarding boots or ski boots if there are plate bindings on the board designed to accommodate them. If you're a skier you may feel more comfortable learning with this setup, although it is not recommended. Make sure the board is a freestyle or freeride model. Alpine and racing boards are too stiff and unforgiving for beginners.

Make sure your rental boots are in good condition. Most importantly — make sure they fit snugly without your toes hitting the end. Loose boots will not provide the necessary support.

Freestyle

Snowboards
In general, there are three types of snowboards.

Freestyle
Freestyle boards have a curved tip and tail. They are shorter, lighter and more flexible than other styles. They are easier to turn and make very good beginner boards. Most boards are freestyle boards. Chances are your rental will be a freestyle. They usually come with freestyle or step-in bindings that require soft boots. This is also the board advanced riders use for jumps, halfpipe and tricks.

Alpine
Alpine carving or racing boards have a curved tip and a flatter tail. They are stiff and not very flexible in order to hold high speed carving turns. Plate bindings and hard

boots are necessary. These models are for advanced riders.

Freeride

Freeride boards combine freestyle and alpine characteristics in order to

Alpine
Waide

create an all-purpose board. Nose and tail are moderately curved. They are moderately flexible as well. They are easier to turn than alpine boards but still capable of holding an edge at high speed. Not bad for beginners. They take freestyle, step-in or plate bindings. This is the board to use if the beginner chooses to wear hard boots with plate or step-in bindings.

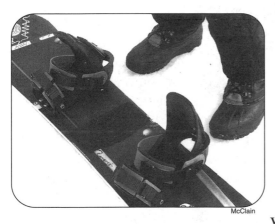
McClain

Bindings

In general, there are three types of bindings:

Freestyle

Freestyle or highback bindings have been the most popular bindings for years. They have high backs that provide support to riders who wear soft boots. They come with two or three straps. These bindings are commonly used with freestyle and freeride boards.

Plate

Plate bind-
ings secure
hard boots
to alpine,
racing or
f r e e r i d e
boards.

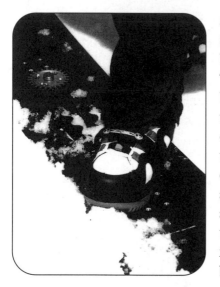

Step-in

Step-in bindings are becoming more popular. The boot has part of the binding device built into the sole which snaps onto the board. Nothing to strap or buckle. They're easy to get in and out of and some models can be adjusted anywhere, anytime. There are step-ins for both soft and hard boots.

Binding Angles and Stance Width

There are a number of ways to adjust bindings. Adjusting the angle of your bindings and the width between them are two of the most important. These adjustments depend in large part on the boot/binding setup you choose.

Soft Boot Setting

The front binding should angle a tad toward the front of the board about 20 to 30 degrees. The rear binding should be adjusted closer to a right angle to the length of the board — approximately 5 to 15 degrees. The distance between the bindings or stance width should be shoulder width — about 20–22 inches. Bindings should be screwed down tight.

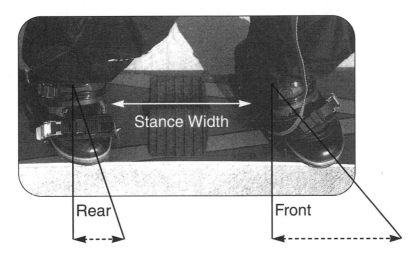

Often the rear-foot binding is angled less than the front-foot binding in order to provide more leverage. It's a good idea when you're starting out. The chart below indicates general settings that the rider may refine according to individual style and need.

Setup	Stance Width	Front Binding Angle	Rear Binding Angle
Soft Boots	20–22 Inches	5–15 Degrees	20–30 Degrees
Hard Boots	16–18 Inches	Angle each binding so there is no toe or heel drag.	

Hard Boot Setting

Hard boots provide more leverage than soft boots. As a result, expert riders enjoy quicker, more powerful edging capabilities. For this setup, angle the bindings so there is no toe or heel drag. The stance width between plate bindings is about 16 to 18 inches. It should be noted that hard boots transmit any and all lower body movement immediately to the snowboard. They are not recommended for beginners because they are not forgiving in that respect. Make a mistake with these puppies and you're down. There is no time to recover.

Secure your feet and see how it feels. Remember, you'll have a natural inclination to put one or the other foot forward. Right foot forward is called "goofy foot" for no real reason and left foot forward is called "regular foot" for no real reason. Just do what feels right for you.

Which Foot Forward?

Here are some hints:

● Use the same stance you would on a skateboard, single water ski or surfboard.

● Use the same stance you would if swinging a golf club or baseball bat.

● Use the same foot forward you would if sliding on a slippery surface (like on your kitchen floor in stocking feet).

● And for you gymnasts: Use the same foot forward you would if executing cartwheels.

Make sure you understand how the bindings work. In order to use the lifts, you'll be taking your back foot out of its binding in order to walk around, get on and off the lifts and skate. In a day of snowboarding that will add up to a lot of in and out, so get good at it.

Your board must have a leash or safety strap. This attaches to your front leg and prevents a runaway board. A loose s n o w b o a r d hurtling down the slope is a death missile. You won't get on the lifts without it.

Barking Dogs (Aching Feet!)

You may suffer aches and pains in your feet and legs at first. It's probably from using

McClain

Recommended: Freestyle board and soft boots. Easier to learn (forgiving!).

and overusing new muscles, but it might be from ill fitting boots and bindings. You want the gear snug but not so tight that it cuts circulation. Try loosening straps and buckles. If the footwear simply doesn't fit, go back to the rental shop and try another pair. Or you might be unconsciously trying to grip the board with your feet. Clawing with your toes will give you heinous cramps. Relax and let the board do as much of the work as possible. Stick with one pair of outer socks.

Final Tips, Reminders, Recommendations

● Standing on its tail, your board should reach approximately from your collarbone to your nose in length.

● Most beginners should start with a freestyle or freeride board. These boards are easier to maneuver than the alpine or racing boards, which are designed for expert riders and high speed carving.

● Wear soft boots with highback bindings (either freestyle or step-in) if you've never skied. Soft boots are more forgiving than hard boots.

● Many skiers want to learn in hard boots. It's not a good idea at first because they do not allow room for error. However, if you insist, you will need plate or step-in bindings. Just make sure you're board is not an alpine or racing model.

Chapter Four:

Carpet Riding

It's very smart to get used to your equipment and practice basic moves before you drive up. You can make adjustments to your gear easily, and your muscles will begin to learn how to carry out the new demands. The latter is called muscle memory and you cannot acquire that soon enough.

Look at it this way: If you don't do it in the comfort of your home, you'll have to do it up there in the snow. If you carpet ride the evening before you depart for the mountains, you'll

The snowboarder's stance is a relaxed ready position. Note that Alison leads with her hands. Knees are slightly flexed with a bit more weight over the front foot.

be the best student in snowboarding class the next day and the apple of your instructor's eye.

Basic Moves

Before you begin, spread something over the carpet to protect it from the wax on the bottom of your snowboard. Make sure you have some room to move.

Secure Your Front Foot

First you must determine which foot you want forward. Secure that foot and place the other on the stomp pad next to the rear binding.

Athletic Stance

Assume an athletic stance: face forward in the direction of the tip of your board (chest in the same direction), arms and hands in front about waist level, knees slightly flexed with more of your weight (approximately 60 to 70%) over the front foot.

It's a part of you now!

Lift, Touch Tip and Tail

Get a feel for your new appendage. Simply lift the board straight up a few inches and touch the tip to the carpet and then the tail.

Walking

The ridiculous angle of your front foot will drive you nuts at first. Slide the board forward about a step and catch up with your free foot. Keep your feet together and take smallish steps to avoid the splits. Try going backward.

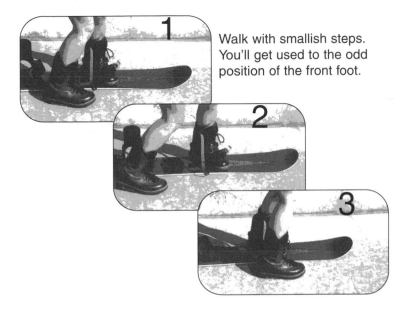

Walk with smallish steps.
You'll get used to the odd
position of the front foot.

Down and up (flex and extend).

Lift and Pivot
Lift the board and pivot yourself around. You can do it in several steps by lifting and repositioning the board by degrees or by lifting once and hopping around on your free foot.

Secure the Other Foot
Now try these movements with both feet secure.

Weighting / Unweighting (Up and Down Movements)
Flex the knees and weight down, then extend up and forward.

Heel-side ...

Upper Body Rotation
Simply pivot the upper body left and right.

Edging
With a chair or wall for support, roll the board on its toe-side edge and its heel-side edge.

Little Jumps
Flex the knees and hop up and down and side to side.

Fore and Aft Movements
Shift your center of mass forward and back.

and toe-side edging.

1-2-3 Turn!

Essential ingredients to turning:
1: Flex
2: Extend forward
3: Rotate.
These movements will pop up again when we move to the mountains.

There you go. These are some of the fundamental moves involved in snowboarding 101. Work these out and your mind and body will be ready for the real thing.

Fore and aft movements.

Chapter Five:

Preparations

Shop, Beg and Borrow

Snowboarding isn't cheap. Mountains aren't free and gear is expensive. You can rent board and boots for now, but you'll have to buy suitable clothing if you can't borrow. Lift tickets, lessons (strongly recommended), travel (for most) and food all add up. In order to rent a snowboard, you'll need to lay down a bunch of cash, a credit card or your next of kin.

So it's important to shop for the closest ski area and the best deals on tickets, rentals and lessons. That means asking around. Using the yellow pages and calling here and there. Borrow as much gear as you can. A little planning and prep will save you major dollars.

Shopping Hints

A good time to buy your own gear is toward the end of the season. You'll find terrific deals on new and used gear (that's when resorts will sell their old rentals). If you plan on doing a lot of boarding, purchase a season pass since this is much cheaper than buying day to day.

Allow for Time

Allow for all the snafus. They will occur. Your first days on the slopes will be very long and tiring. Don't add to the frustrations by running late for lessons. Leave early for the mountains. Don't believe them when they say the drive is only 2 hours. Give yourself an extra hour. Believe me — it'll take time to find the place, park, buy tickets, rent gear and put it all on. You'll be amazed at how long it takes to lace and buckle your boots with freezing fingers.

Good Times to Go

Expect a suitable base for snowboarding from November through April in the northern hemisphere. The season is longer or shorter depending on altitude, location, and specific weather conditions. The season is reversed (June to October) in the southern hemisphere.

Early and late in the season can be great. Spring is a particularly good time to go because everybody thinks summertime thoughts. The slopes aren't crowded, the snow is soft and you can board with less clothing. Christmas vacation is nuts, of course. Anytime after fresh snow is good. Keep tabs on the weather.

Final Check

Before you begin your journey to the mountains, consider a number of things.

❏ Call ahead for conditions and check the forecast. Make sure the roads are clear. You may need chains, cables or snow tires. Better ask. Cables work about as well as chains. Remember that everything costs more in the mountains if you can get it at all.

❏ Make sure the snow has a good foundation. You can't learn on ice.

❏ Bring extra clothing. You'll need to change.

❏ Bring your own food. Dining at the lodge can be expensive and less than stellar. Good food for a day of snowboarding begins with protein and includes complex carbohydrates that will maintain blood sugar. For example, have an oatmeal or egg breakfast and eat cereal bar snacks throughout the day.

❏ Bring plenty of water. Exercise and alpine conditions will create a big thirst. It's best to avoid caffeine and alcoholic drinks since they actually inhibit hydration.

❏ Get plenty of sleep.

❏ Make sure you know where you're going. Bring a map.

❏ Bring money and credit cards for rentals, emergencies, incidentals, and bribes (on crowded days you may be able to slip the parking attendant a few bucks to get a good parking spot).

❏ Remember all your gear.

❏ Tank up before you go up. Check oil, water and tire pressure, too.

❏ Bring your enthusiasm.

If Tripping Up for the First Time
You go up the mountain on winding, often dangerous roads. You are forever looking in your rear view mirror to check for tailgaters or trying to find a way to pass the slowpoke ahead of you. It's wise to drive cautiously up there. Use the turnouts and let the impatient ones pass. Relax and enjoy the scenery. You'll arrive soon enough.

It's a long way down if you take that one hairpin too fast (yet fools do it all the time). Watch out for rocks in the road. Some are sharp and some are bigger than you think. Run over a bad one and you may suffer a flat and/or damage to your undercarriage. It happens!

There's the turnoff. You drive into a big parking area full of folks getting dressed for snowboarding or skiing (if it's crowded you'll have to park somewhere else and shuttle in — another reason to get up early). Many are listening to very loud car stereos as they prepare. Next to the parking lot is a cluster of buildings that make up a resort: ticket windows, rental shop, offices, restaurant, bathrooms and retail shops. Look up and see the lifts stretching up the mountain over the slopes and all the teeny tiny riders zooming down (Wow!). It's thrilling to think that you'll soon be doing that!

Now it's time to play window bingo. Buy your lift tickets here, your lesson ticket there and your rentals (if you haven't rented somewhere else) down the stairs and around to your left, behind the restaurant. Some ski areas may be more convenient than others, but make sure you have given yourself plenty of time to get lost.

When you buy your lift ticket, make sure you get the wire hooking device that attaches the ticket to you. They'll be hanging in bunches next to the window. The ticket is printed on sticky back paper. Peel off the backing and fold it over the fat end of the wire AFTER you hook the wire through the loop of something you're going to wear all day. Your ticket needs to be seen plainly in order to use the lifts. If you need to change the piece of clothing you've hooked your ticket to, go back to the window or to guest relations for a fresh ticket.

If you need to rent gear, find the rental shop and get fitted for boots and board. Make sure the fit is good and the boots aren't too mangled. Check out the board. Make sure the bindings are intact and that you understand how to use them. Make sure you have a leash. Make sure you have a stomp pad between the bindings.

Keep your eye on the clock! Don't be late for your class. Find the place to buy your lesson ticket. Stash your street shoes in a locker or in your car and put on your boots. Lace them snug.

On to your lesson.

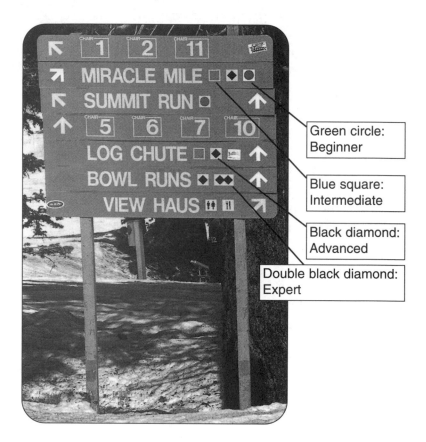

Board Corrals
Locate the board corrals. This is where you can safely stow your snowboard when you need to go inside to eat or pee.

Important Signs
Signs mean a great deal up there.

Daily Conditions
A big sign next to the ticket windows indicates what the day's snow and weather will be like.

Map of Trails
A big sign of the mountain should be centrally located indicating the lifts and the degree of difficulty and location of all the ski trails. Make sure you get the pocket map that shows all that stuff. Have an eye out for signs that indicate which lifts are in operation and where they are located.

Trail Signs
These are the all-important signs located at all the trail heads on the slopes. These signs point the way and indicate the degree of difficulty of trails down the mountain.

● Beginner = green circle

■ Intermediate = blue square

◆ Advanced = black diamond

◆◆ Expert = double black diamond

But This Time I'm Not Fooling!
Treks on and off the mountains can be tricky no matter how well you plan. My pal Stu, for example, still has his neck hairs standing on end over this incident.

First of all, you have to understand Stu. Stu is the kind of guy who will call you up impersonating the IRS. Hardy har har har. Big joker. He's world-famous for his practical jokes and has got us all with zingers, pranks and 1,001 other minor annoyances.

Anyway, Stu's driving his truck down the mountain after a long day of snowboarding. Six guys are piled in the back. It's freezing.

All of a sudden Stu shouts I DON'T HAVE ANY BRAKES!

Nobody believes him of course. After all, he's the cut up, right? But, hey, nice try, Stu.

So picture this. It's dark, cold, and the truck is careening down the steepest grade of the peak . . . going faster and faster. Stu is going nuts because there REALLY AREN'T ANY BRAKES, and he's starting to think that EVERY-BODY IS GOING TO DIE.

And no one believes him.

But the man prevails. He gently coaxes the runaway truck to a halt using the emergency brake. That had to be a chore, because his is one of those really big trucks. By now, everyone is a believer after watching Stu grunt and groan with the hand brake. Each passenger wipes the cold sweat from his brow. (Thank you, Lord!)

Seems the brake calipers actually froze, rendering the foot brake useless. Luckily, the emergency brake didn't suffer the same fate. After dousing the drums with water, the calipers unstuck, and the journey home resumed.

This ditty illustrates the need to respect the mountains in winter. The weather is a force to be reckoned with. Be aware. Especially when you're driving.

Chapter Six:

On the Flats

Find yourself a gently sloping area at the base of your mountain with flat areas above and below. Make sure you're off to the side and away from skiers and other snowboarders.

Secure your front foot and attach the leash. Start the day learning how to fall safely and correctly.

Falling
Absorb toe-side falls by making fists and landing on both knees and both fists. Absorb heel-side falls by rolling from butt to back.

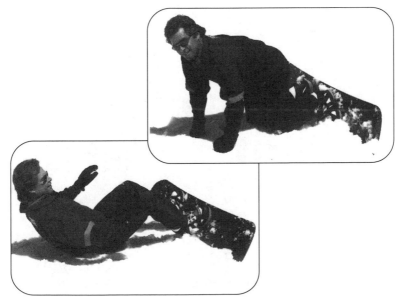

Basic Moves

Go over the basic moves that you drilled at home on the carpet. This is a good warm-up and, of course good practice. This is, after all, the beginning of the real thing.

❑ Athletic Stance
❑ Lift, Touch Tip and Tail
❑ Walking
❑ Lift and Pivot
❑ Weighting and Unweighting
  (Up and Down Movements)
❑ Upper Body Rotation
❑ Edging
❑ Little Jumps
❑ Fore and Aft Movements

Ready position:
Just like you did in the living room. Eyes front, hands point ahead, knees flexed and weight slightly forward.

Lift it. Hop with it. Turn around with it. Get used to life with the ultimate foot extender.

Below: Heel- and toe-side edging. The inset to the right shows on-the-hill application. Oh yeah.

On the Flats

McClain

Walking with the board is awkward at first, but it'll grow on you.
Keep your free foot close to the board and take short steps.

Cover short distances when both feet are strapped by simply flexing your knees and jumping.

McClain

Rotation in action: from practice at home, to the flats, to a real turn on the slope.

Make the connection?

Skating

You'll need to free your rear foot. Digging your free foot into the snow, build up some speed as if you were on a skateboard. Keep your free foot close to the board and take small steps. When you have enough speed to glide, place your free foot on the stomp pad located between the two bindings. Balance yourself with an athletic stance.

Look ahead (not at your feet), place your weight forward over the front foot, flex the knees and place your hands in front (not at your sides) about waist-high. You are relaxed, comfortable and in control. It's like riding a bike. Once you feel it — you got it.

Practice skating (on the flats) pushing off from both sides of the board. This will get you into the habit of keeping most of your weight over the front foot, where it should be.

Walking Up a Hill

Advance up the gentle slope with your free foot in the lead and your boarded foot at right angles to the slope. Position the board sideways to the slope and dig the uphill edge into the snow. Push off the anchored board and take a small step up the hill with your free foot. Lift the board, keeping it at right angles to the slope and bring it alongside your free foot. Repeat until you've reached the level you want.

Place your rear foot toe over the edge of your board and use it to help you brake.

Sliding: Your first runs are just little trips down a small hill. The rear foot is loose and rests on the stomp pad next to the rear binding. Knees are flexed, weight is forward and your hands are out front pointing the way. Wheeee!

On a Small Hill

Your First Runs

Learn about downhill riding in small increments. Begin by hiking five feet up a small slope. Turn around and place your free foot on the stomp pad with the toe of your boot overhanging the edge. Assume the snow-boarder's stance and let the board slide down. Always look ahead. Place your hands in front and position your weight forward.

Let your overhanging toe drag you to a kind of turning stop. As you're doing this toe dragging, point your arms and rotate your body in the direction of your mini-turn. Turning into the hill will help you slow and stop along with your toe.

Increase the length of your descent five feet each time. Make several runs practicing toe drag and upper body rotation. It's important to learn how to ride your board with your rear foot free because this is how you'll get off the lift.

Zen Note

As you zoom down, feel yourself **over** the board. Feel yourself **over** the speeding hill. Feel the mountain directly **underneath** the soles of your feet.

Sideslipping

Sideslipping is riding downhill with the snowboard at a right angle to the fall line. Climb up the training hill and place the snowboard across the slope. Facing downhill, get the board to slip or skid sideways by rolling forward on your feet. Do not allow the board to lie flat. This will cause your downhill edge to catch and you'll fall.

Look in the direction you want to go. Place your hands in front. Control your downhill progress by lifting your toes and rocking back on your heels to slow or stop. After practicing the heel-side slip, try going toe-side (facing uphill).

Sideslipping is the safe and sure way to negotiate terrain that you may find difficult. No matter how steep the grade you can comfortably sideslip your way down the mountain.

Diagonal Sideslipping

Diagonal sideslipping is simply slipping downhill at an angle you choose. It helps to reach with your arms and to point where you want to go. You control your progress the same way you do a straight sideslip. Apply more pressure on the uphill edge to slow down and slight pressure on your downhill edge to speed up. Knees are flexed and your weight forward. Work with your ankles. Again, it's very important that the snowboard never lay flat on the slope. As soon as it does it will dig its downhill edge and you will slam. Always ride the uphill edge.

Practice diagonal sideslips by climbing 30 feet or so up the hill. Aim diagonally across the hill, assume an athletic

Sideslipping instills confidence: It'll get you down anything short of a cliff. It's a major point of learning that leads directly to more advanced technique.

stance, place your rear foot on the stomp pad and go. When you reach the bottom, climb straight up so you can practice your slips in the opposite direction.

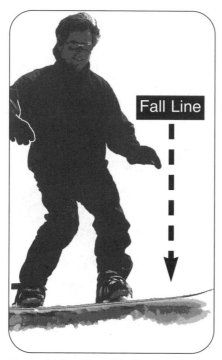

Jim rolls back on his heels to execute a heel-side stop.

About Stopping

It isn't like skiing. It takes awhile to neatly stop, relax and remain standing on the slopes. The board wants to move. Since you're strapped in on one instead of two separate things, maintaining your balance is almost impossible at first. So, if you really want to stop and stay put on the slopes, sit on your can.

As you learn more about edge control your ability to stop will improve dramatically. We'll get into that in the next chapter. Right now you should be sliding on a teeny little hill at the base of which you can more or less glide to a halt with the help of a dragging toe.

You can slow down and stop (sort of) after you slide by rolling back on your heels or up on your toes and digging your UPHILL EDGE. Then you'll flap your arms wildly and fall down. Since stopping is iffy at this point,

I think ...

I'm going ...

too fast!

Braaake!!!!

Cruising

From a somewhat out of control slide our guy neatly executes a toe-side stop in order to rethink his downhill trek.

He opts for a heel-side sideslip.

Nice hat.

it's a really good idea to stay away from everybody and everything.

More About Falling Down

This you'll get good at. And that's OK. Everybody wipes out. You just don't want to get hurt, of course. Stay away from the difficult trails until you know how to deal with them. And try to avoid catching your downhill edge. Again, edges are the sides of the snowboard. Catching your downhill edge means that you will fall downhill hard and fast. That's why they call it slamming. Uphill falls are much easier to take. The distance is shorter to fall and recovering from them is simpler.

Up to now, you've been taking very short runs down a bunny slope. If you fall, it's probably because you simply lost your balance and the falls should be relatively mild. Just make sure your hands are balled up in fists if you fall toe-side ... and that you roll from butt to back if you fall heel-side. If your rear foot is unsecured, keep it on the board as you fall.

As you travel up the slopes and try new things you'll self-destruct in any number of unique and interesting ways. I've included a number of photos illustrating various recovery techniques for fun and games.

But don't let the wipeouts get you down! It's a part of the process and EVERYBODY takes spills. In fact, if you're not falling down at all you're probably not risking enough in your training.

Easy Does It

A special note about the dynamics of our sport. Gravity

Fall Line

McClain

The uphill faceplant is a relatively easy fall to take and recover from. There's less distance to fall and scrambling to your knees isn't difficult. In all recoveries it's important to keep the board at right angles to the fall line until you're ready to slide.

pulls you down lickety-split on a snowy slope when you're attached to a snowboard. The steeper the hill, the faster you go. And boy, it's a lot faster than you think if you've never tried it. That's what makes this sport so much fun. Flying down the face of a mountain is one of those living-in-the-moment experiences we sometimes have and should have a heck of a lot more of.

But when you first try the sport, you cannot deal with much steepness without serious consequences. Without practice and training, sliding down even a beginner's slope is like running across the freeway. It's important to be bold as you learn, but not foolhardy. Build your skills patiently so that when you do find yourself in the land of steepness you can ride it out with poise and self assurance.

Case in Point
Doug's legendary first 45 minutes on a snowboard:

I slammed into the mountain about six times — twice on my back, twice on my face, twice in another way I don't want to talk about. I cracked a rib. I got whiplash. I knocked the wind out of myself each time. The pain was one thing, but worse was the fatigue. All that pounding just sapped me. I never fully recovered that day. I can't remember ever being so trashed.

Too much speed plus too little training equals mishap. Every snowboarder I know has a first-day story about horrific falls and eating painkillers. Like it's part of the plan or something. Looking back, I wish I had eased up on the testosterone and spent more time on easier trails (with a good instructor!). I would have learned faster

The uphill buttplant is another minor fall.

Inset (2): It helps to grab the board toward the tip with your rear hand to help you up.

McClain

McClain

The downhill faceplant is another matter. This and the downhill buttplant are usually the result of catching your downhill edge and slamming.

The downhill buttplant is often a real head banger. It's the hardest fall to recover from as well. Dig the tail, roll over and scoot up.

McClain

and enjoyed the learning experience more.

Take it easy your first day. Take lessons. Work on the basics in a forgiving environment with a forgiving attitude about yourself. I honestly think you can learn this sport without killing yourself. This is a revolutionary concept in some circles, but hey ... why don't you prove me right.

Lifts

Up the Mountain

You'll need a little speed and a real slope to acquaint yourself properly with intermediate snowboarding technique. The small training hill was good for assimilating simple sliding techniques, but it doesn't provide the gravitational pull or run-length you'll need to learn the real thing.

Find a beginner trail. Usually such trails are marked by a green circle. As opposed to a blue square (intermediate) or a black diamond (advanced). What you want is a hill with enough steepness to get you going but not so much as to ignite any vertigo. Too much hill fosters overcompensation (flailing arms, overturning) and faceplants. But first you must negotiate the lifts.

Using the Lifts
When using the lifts, be alert and pay attention to the attendants. Tell them you're new to the sport and they will help you.

Getting On
Join the lift line at the end. It's polite not to stomp on others equipment. Try to get a seat by yourself. It'll make unloading more manageable.

As soon as the chair in front of yours swoops by, scoot up to the loading area. Look behind you and to the out-side. Make sure your butt is aimed toward the middle of the advancing chair. As you get scooped up, grab hold of the chair.

Face forward and lift the nose of your snowboard. If your board digs into the snow here, you will either dismount hard and fast or leave a leg. Settle your weight in a balanced way on the seat. Now is a good time to kick off any snow stuck on your board. Resting the board on your free foot helps to ease its dangling weight. Enjoy the view!

Arrive well ahead of the advancing chair. Aim your butt for the middle of the seat.

As the chair picks you up grab hold and settle back. If there's a safety bar, bring it down into place.

McClain

Getting Off

Truly one of the more humbling experiences in all of sports. As your chair dips down into the unloading area, POINT YOUR BOARD STRAIGHT AHEAD with the tip up. Position your free foot on the stomp pad. You should be sitting forward. As your board hits the snow assume the snowboarder's stance. The momentum of the lift should be just enough to gently shove you down the (hopefully) slight incline. Glide to a halt if you can. You may have to drag a toe and gradually increase pressure. This will slow you down and turn you slightly. If you fall, get up immediately and skate out of the unloading zone.

Common Mistakes

● Board is not pointed forward.
● Back foot comes off board.
● Leaning back after dismounting.

Good Practice

When you start making runs down the mountain you can practice unloading technique by stopping several feet above the flats at the base of the hill and pretend your getting off a lift. Take your rear foot out of its binding, place it on the stomp pad and use your toe to monitor your speed.

We've All Been There

Unloading can be a nightmare for snowboarders. Early in my snowboarding experience, I was at Heavenly, a wonderful resort next to Lake Tahoe, where I set a record for stumbling dismounts. I ate it three times in a row getting off the express lift and all three times the lift operator had to shut the lift down while I crawled out of the way. Of course, I was finally chastised by the operator (*Dude!*

I can't keep shutting down the mountain just for you!) and was so humiliated that to this day I cringe the tiniest bit each time a chair whisks me up the hill. I prepare myself for the unloading by visualizing a graceful exit.

Point the board straight!

Remember your sliding stance? Eyes front, hands point the way, knees flexed and weight forward.

Toe drag will turn you toe-side.

That first ride down is a tangy blend
of exhilaration and terror. Yee-haw!

Chapter Nine:

Down the Mountain

I Can't Go Down That!

OK, you're on top of a beginner's slope. If it's your first time, you'll be amazed at how steep it is (OH, NO!), but you will get over that. You just need to build your confidence. And in order to do that, you need to know how to control the stick strapped to your feet.

Buckle Up

Secure both feet. You'll probably have to sit on your can to do this although there might be a bench to sit on. The vicinity of the unloading area should be pretty flat, so sitting down, securing and standing back up shouldn't be a problem. Strap in close to the slope.

If you're on a slope, sit facing downhill so that the board lies across the fall line. After securing both feet, get up by grabbing the downhill edge of your board with your rear hand (the hand on the same side as your rear foot, remember the labels?). It helps to grab toward the tip. Pull and straighten your legs.

You can make the job easier by shoving snow with your board (while sitting and facing downhill) and building a platform. Now you have a level place to secure your binding and to stand.

If you're not in the immediate vicinity of the downhill grade, you can hop to it with both feet secured. If this isn't working, you must free your rear foot and walk or skate closer to the slope.

More Sideslipping
Start with sideslips. Sideslipping is your ace-in-the-hole on the hill. You can always sideslip to safety.

Position your board across the fall line. Assume an athletic posture. Always look in the direction you want to go. Hands in front. Point at your target. Practice rolling forward to accelerate and rolling back to slow down. Relax. Legs are slightly flexed. Smile. You're in control.

Falling Leaf
When you alternate diagonal sideslips (slipping to your left, to your right, back to your left, and so on) you are executing the falling leaf. The name comes from the movement a leaf can make as it falls off a tree and wafts to and fro down to earth. Using this technique your board can make similar tracks all the way down the trail.

From a sideslip, shift some weight to the front (nose or tip) or rear (tail) of the board. You will begin to drift in that direction. It might take a long second for the weight

Anatomy of the Falling Leaf

Alternate directional sideslips and you create a falling leaf.

Some folks are happy to stay at this level for a while. It's not high performance, but it'll get you down the hill.

shift to take effect. Keep smiling. You're still in control. You're starting to ride!

Common Mistakes

- Going to fast! Gently put more pressure on the uphill edge to slow down.
- Jerky movements. Quiet your upper body movement and apply subtle ankle movements instead.

Diagonal Sideslips

When you execute the falling leaf, you'll probably come close to doing some diagonal sideslipping. You see, it's all connected.

Begin your diagonal sideslip by shifting your weight forward toward the tip of your board and in the direction you want to go. Reach and point with hands and arms. Away you'll go!

Control your speed by pressuring your uphill edge to slow down. Speed up by easing pressure on the uphill edge. Stop by rotating your upper body into the hill, turning up the slope and setting your uphill edge.

Pressuring the uphill edge to slow down.

Practice going both ways, toe-side and heel-side. After traversing across the trail in one direction, you'll need to sit down, roll over and point your tip in the other direction (when you learn how to turn, you'll never have to do this again!).

Anatomy of a Diagonal Sideslip

Fall Line

Diagonal sideslips are relatively easy to control. Just pressure the uphill edge to slow or stop.

Until you know how to turn you'll have to sit down and roll over in order to go the other way.

Common Mistakes
● Dropping hands.
● Leaning back, resulting in a backward drift.

Garlands

When a rider traverses in one direction across the fall line, then steers uphill to slow and then drops down into a traverse again, he has executed a garland. A series of such partial turns and drops during a traverse leaves a droopy track on the slope much like a garland makes on a Christmas tree, hence the name. Garlands are a terrific way to practice turning technique without transferring edges. This is one of the last exercises to master before a rider tackles one of the major levels of competence in snowboarding — linking toe-side and heel-side turns.

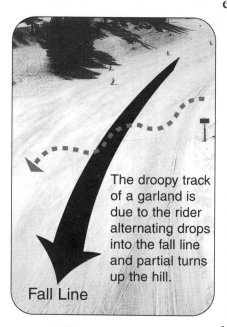

The droopy track of a garland is due to the rider alternating drops into the fall line and partial turns up the hill.

Fall Line

Start your traverse, pressure the uphill edge of your board and go up the hill almost to stop. Then look downhill, rise up and forward and flatten your board. The board will begin to seek the fall line. Once it does, look ahead, bend your knees and put pressure back on your uphill edge to slow down. You should be flexed and ready to repeat. Try at least three or four turns during each traverse. Go both ways in order to practice heel- and toe-side turns.

Anatomy of a Garland

Fall Line

1: Seeking the fall line and gathering speed.
2: Pressuring the uphill edge and slowing.
3: Rotating the body downhill
4: Seeking the fall line once again.

Common mistakes

● Catching downhill edge.
● Dropping hands and leaning back.
● Going too fast (although some speed is required to break through snow).
● Looking down at the board and not ahead.

More Zen

Now you're getting a taste of riding. Not just sliding down. You're directing your travel. You're controlling it. Feel yourself riding with your board. It's a part of you. Weight forward is key. It keeps you over your board and on top of the journey. Moderate your speed. Flow from one move to the next.

Connections

Do you see the connections? These exercises seem somewhat distinct from one another on the page, but in reality one flows into the other. The basic moves you practiced on the carpet are the common threads that connect all the snowboarding skills up to this point. They are simply developed and refined from one stage to the next.

Having Fun?

If you've mastered everything so far, congratulations! And welcome to the mountain. Because now you can go down almost any trail if you have to. Even a black diamond if you happen to find yourself on one by mistake (it happens) and must wend your way down.

If you know how to sideslip, diagonally sideslip and make garlands you are ready to enjoy the slopes. Many are satisfied to remain at this level for awhile — and why not? If you're having fun that's all that matters.

No Problem. I Sideslip

My first real appreciation for the sideways skid occurred my second day of snowboarding. Somehow my buddy and I got lost. It was nearly closing time and we were both very, very tired.

Luckily, we stumbled upon a skier who was happy to show us the way back to the parking lot. I remember staggering over to the edge of the final descent and looking down at my worst nightmare. It was absolutely vertical and littered with moguls.

It was pretty scary. But being the he-men we were, we turned our boards at right angles to the sheer drop and sideslipped all ... the ... way ... down. Not very dashing. But healthy.

Beating the fear monster is one of the first things you gotta do as you learn. And you can do that by riding sideways. Learn how to sideslip.

Riding on the (Correct) Edge

Flying straight down the hill is thrilling, sure. But in order to have any kind of control over the snowboard, you must learn how to turn and traverse both ways. In this chapter you've been building up to that. In the next chapter you'll find out more about turning.

Whenever you turn or traverse on a slope, edges play an important part of your movement. As mentioned before, edges refer to the sides of your snowboard.

Except during the nano-second when you transfer edges during a turn, never ride your board flat on the snow.

As a rule you always ride the uphill edge. The uphill edge is the side of the snowboard facing, or closest to facing, uphill. The downhill edge faces downhill. Even when it seems like a rider is riding straight down on the flat of his board, he is in fact favoring the uphill edge.

You cannot ride your downhill edge. As soon as it touches snow it will catch and slam you down.

Don't Do This, OK?
This is how I learned about edges.

Without a clue as to what snowboarding was all about, I took a lift up my first hill. It wasn't very steep really. I look at it now and laugh. But at the time it may as well have been the Matterhorn.

My so-called instructor (no names) went down the hill first. He stopped at the bottom and waved me down. *Go this way and then go that way* he shouted, waving his arms this way and that way. *Let's work on your turns.*

Shoving off, I went *this way* fine. Smooth, in fact. My stance felt right and I held out my arms like a real shred-master. Man, I must have looked sharp. Going *that way* was a problem though. My instructor was waving and yelling *Turn! Turn!* but I realized I simply had no idea how to crank this sucker around. It was going straight for the trees and I could not locate the steering wheel.

When I opened my eyes I saw nothing but blue sky and stars. My head was buried in a foot of snow. My lungs were collapsed and my neck was starting to swell. My instructor boarded up to my body and asked if I was all right. I immediately answered in the affirmative although that was *not* the case.

He announced to the rest of the class *This is what happens when you catch an edge. Don't catch your edge, OK?*

Learning about things can happen in many ways. You can stick your hand into a flame and learn about heat. You can run across the freeway and learn about car velocity. You can jump into a lion's cage and learn about teeth. You can learn about snowboarding the hard way, too. It does make for some interesting stories (if you survive). But trust me on this. There is a more intelligent (huh?) way to go about it.

(tweet tweet)

There will be moments of doubt throughout your learning curve.

McClain

Before you go any further, check out your basic form. Diagonal Sideslips and garlands are the bridges to turning. Are you looking like this?

Classic Form

The stance is based on an athletic ready position.

1: Looking, *always looking* where you want to go.
2: Shoulders, chest and hips face target destination.
3: Hands held up and out, literally pointing the way.
4: Knees are slightly flexed and ready to roll into turns.
5: Weight is positioned somewhat forward toward the tip.

Chapter Ten:

Turns !

Turning is a basic function of down-hill travel, but can be a higher form of art when mind, body and mountain meet in concert on the edge of a snowboard.

When you're ready to get more out of your snowboard and your riding experience it's time to learn how to turn.

Basic Turns

The garland exercises taught you how to execute the beginnings of a turn. You're not that far away from turning if you're a garlandmeister.

Here's the lowdown, step by step:

Begin your traverse as if you're about to execute a series of garlands. Make the partial turn up the hill and slow down as before. You should be in the flexed position.

1: In an athletic stance, look where you want to go with your hands held out in front. Remember your body will tend to follow your hands.

2: Rise up and extend your body toward the tip of your board.

3: Let the board flatten a bit on the surface of the hill. Keep your weight slightly forward and let the tip begin to drift down the fall line. This is when most people start to lean back. Don't do that! You are already about halfway through your turn.

4: Keep looking in the direction of your turn and rotate your upper body in that direction. Follow this with active leg and feet steering.

5: Lightly pressure the new edge of your board as you come around and bend your knees. Your weight may come back to the center of the board but not over the rear foot.

6: Assume a flexed position and continue the turn until you slow down.

You are now in position to try a basic turn the other way. Follow the same steps in the new direction.

Guess what? You've just linked your turns.

The Formula

Up+Forward+Flatten+Wait+Rotate+Bend = Turn!
Extend yourself **Up.**
Lean **Forward.**
Flatten your board on the snow.
Wait for the tip of your board to find Mr. Fall Line.
Rotate your body in the direction of the turn.
Bend your knees.

Seriously! Copy and tape these instructions on your wrist. Highly skilled professional quarterbacks do it, why not you?

Anatomy of a Toe-side

Take a good look at the form in these images. They are reflections of all the moves you've been practicing from the carpet to the hill: Flex, extend, rotate. Eyes front, hands pointing the way, weight forward.

Anatomy of a Heel-side Turn

Rotation starts with a turn of the head. The arms and upper body turn next, and like a twisting rubber band, induce the lower body including feet and board to come around.

Note

A snowboard is not designed to turn like a surfboard or water ski. You can't muscle through the turn. That's probably why it's so difficult for most beginners to get the feeling right away. But once you get it, your muscles will remember.

More Zen

This is riding. You are face to face with the counterintuitive each time you release the uphill edge and angle downhill to set up a turn. Reach into your turns and embrace the gravity. Lead with your rotating upper body. Your center is forward and always over the board. Think smooth transitions from edge to edge. The sweet spot is always out ahead. Never back.

Common Mistakes

● Too much edge too soon. Edge digs in and you fall.

● Rotating the body too soon. Let the board design do some of the work.

● Throughout the turn your unconscious mind is telling you to gradually lean back. However, this transfers your weight to the tail of the board and soon you'll be out of control.

● Dropping hands. Think of reaching and pointing where you want to go.

● Going too fast. Finish every turn to slow down and keep control. Don't let the board control you.

After Basic Turns

Practice linking your basic turns. At first blend your heel-side and toe-side turns in large arcs concentrating on smooth, graceful transitions. As you feel more confident, try making the arcs smaller and the traverses between turns shorter.

After getting these turns down, begin to use less upper body rotation and start to let the board do more of the work. Use the edge and spring off of it to help you get into your turns. When you're in sync with the board and comfortable with the technique, your downhill journey will become almost effortless.

Steepness

Deal with the hill in increments. Sometimes looking all the way down a new trail makes it seem so vast and deep. Ride the hill one turn at a time. Concentrate on the area where you plan to execute the new turn. This will ease trepidation and make the ride more manageable.

Visualization

Dream about the perfect ride ...

Turn, turn, turn! Edge-to-edge, feeling yourself lean down the hill, freeing your edges and rolling from one to the other in a rhythmic, athletic manner. Never losing control or falling down.

The steepness is tricky and requires that your weight remain somewhat forward as you sail downhill. Transitions are crisp and confident. There's no lagging. You never miss a beat with a transition. You are in perfect harmony with the board and the terrain.

Turning at will defines solid riding ability. It's a whole new plateau of control and fun.

Heel-side

Toe-side

Dream on this. Smoothly sweeping from one edge to the other is like flying.

Linked!

Turns!

Video
With friend and camera you can videotape each other as you learn. This provides 100% unadulterated feedback as well as laughs for years to come. Not advised for those with large, overly sensitive egos.

Fakie
Now learn how to do all this stuff backwards (no kidding!). It primes you for freestyle riding (if that's where you want to go) and can get you out of some tricky situations. Yes, it's do-able.

Turning too soon:
Probably the all-time leading mistake made by beginners.

Too much edge too soon!
If you rush it chances are you'll dig your edge and fall .

Perfect   Not so good

More form:

The rider on the right is not alone. We see it all the time. In fact, it's recommended **not** to look at other snowboarders as you learn. Mutant form is often the result of imitating the haphazard antics of the wrong riders. Especially those of friends and lovers.

The fellow in the button down is not ready for anything but a fall:

1: Not looking ahead.
2: Shoulders, chest and hips do not face target destination.
3: Arms and hands dropped and held behind.
4: Knees locked.
5: Leaning back.
6: Bent at the waist.

Despite the obvious differences, both riders pictured above are executing exactly the same thing: a heel-side turn. The only

Carving

First Carve

I'd been snowboarding about a week before I made this one particular turn. It's not that I hadn't made a hundred before this one. It's just that this one really felt like, well . . . how I imagined a great turn should feel. I was at Squaw Valley, California. Truly the queen of the Sierras. Vast, swooping slopes. A gigantic bowl that lets you rip at will. I suppose that had something to do with it.

I was straightening out on this one trail. I let my speed build until the trail began to dog leg. Then I rose on my toe-side edge and *carved* a turn. No skidding. No over-turning. Just a perfect cranking turn that seemed to last twice as long as any I ever had.

A turn like that is impossible to describe in words. Every sport has its sweet spots and I guess that was my first with snowboarding. Turning is a basic function of down-hill travel, but can be a higher form of art when mind, body and mountain meet in concert on the edge of a snowboard.

Edge to Edge

A carved turn is one that utilizes a snowboard's edge only. There is no skidding. Riders who are good at it put on a powerful and graceful display. Although the scope of this book is limited to beginning technique, it's only natural to mention the most dramatic (yet logical) exten-sion of turning on a snowboard.

Carving down the mountain is certainly something to look forward to, and once you've mastered the basic turn, it's something you can begin working on. Like everything else up to this point, concentrate on one step at a time.

Basic Technique
● Use a good athletic stance.

● Hands are level with the hill and out in front.

● Make your first carves by making simple traverses and lifting the edge. As you pick up the technique increase your downhill angle.

● Transferring edges: The key is to get on a new edge before the turn, then let the board come around.

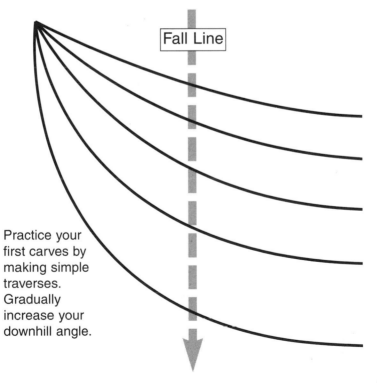

Fall Line

Practice your first carves by making simple traverses. Gradually increase your downhill angle.

Turns!

Carving edge to
edge. Steve allows
his board design to
work the turns.

Interview with an
Instructor's
Instructor

Jim Waide is one of the top snowboard and ski instructors in the country. For four straight years he's been chosen as one of **Skiing Magazine's Top 100 Instructors** in the United States. As an official examiner with the American Association of Snowboard Instructors (AASI) he certifies other instructors in clinics and tests throughout California.

After 25 years on the hill and nearly a decade of teaching experience, Jim has successfully introduced thousands of all ages to the thrills of snowboarding. The following interview provides an enlightening and straightforward account of what you're in for.

How did you first become acquainted with snow-boarding?

It's a family thing. Back in the 40s in Michigan my dad, Douglas Waide, and his friends used to stand and ride on wooden barrel slats they nailed together.

Can a beginner learn to ride in a day?

Yes. Even if he's having a problem with turns, he can still sideslip down the hill and have fun. I've seen students sideslip for days without learning how to turn and still have a blast. Even a novice can go down a steep hill using the sideslipping method.

Do you have to endure a lot of falling as you learn? Is it dangerous?

You will fall a lot but you don't have to get hurt. I've taught thousands of people and only dealt with bruises and maybe an occasional sprain (I've had a few myself!). But never a major injury.

How do you minimize the danger?

By progressively working up to steeper slopes. Like five feet at a time. The problems occur when somebody who knows a little about snowboarding takes a friend who knows nothing to the top of the hill (even a bunny hill) and says *go for it and I'll give you some pointers*. This is a terrible approach! The beginner's fear outweighs his understanding of snowboarding and it becomes a survival thing. If you deal with the steepness incrementally, in manageable chunks, the student can avoid being afraid and concentrate on riding technique. And have fun.

You must be doing something right if you've taught thousands and nobody is getting hurt! Everyone I know, myself included, got destroyed his first day out.

It's the fear factor. When fear sets in, a person gets rigid and leans back. That's the worst thing you can do! You want to stay loose in a good athletic posture with your weight somewhat forward on the snowboard. You can't do that when you're scared stiff!

What are the stages of learning?
Rent equipment before you go up and practice the basic moves at home. At the ski area practice the basic moves again on a flat area. Then try going down small hills or get a lesson. Get a feel for sliding on a slippery surface. Find your balance. Then take the time to learn how to turn. After that you can try the halfpipe, jumping and carving.

What's the time frame for learning linked turns on an intermediate slope?
Anywhere from four to 100 hours (laughter). To link turns at will versus just stumbling in and out of them, I'd say about one to four days.

How does a beginner find good coaching?
Ask for a certified AASI (American Association of Snowboard Instructors) instructor and private lessons. A regular class lesson will be the luck of the draw but reputable ski areas have good instruction at all levels. It should be noted that some areas have better instruction than others. Better ask around!

What kind of boots, board and bindings should a beginner use?
Rent first. Learn on a smallish board, say about chest high as it rests on its tail. A smallish board is safer and easier to turn. Definitely ride a freestyle board with soft boots. Your rental should come with highback bindings for support or, if they're step-in bindings, have stiffeners built into the boot.

Some expert skiers want to jump right away into carving. They're used to hard boots and plate bindings and that's the setup they want to ride in. I would not suggest that. It's too unforgiving and dangerous. It's too easy to catch an edge. Hard boots transmit every little movement to the snowboard. In this setup you don't have time to recover if you make false moves. If you catch an edge you'll slam before you know it.

What's with all the settings for bindings? It's a little confusing.
There are no definite rules or standards. If you've skateboarded or surfed you'll have a comfort range for your angles. That is, the front foot is angled more forward than the back foot. The back foot is still angled but more straight across than the front. Later on you'll adjust according to your style of riding. For example, with hard boots and a carving setup you'll angle your feet dramatically forward. But in the beginning, just angle the front foot out a bit more than the back. That's probably where you'll feel most comfortable and you'll have more leverage for balance and turning.

What kind of condition should a beginner be in? Do you have to be in good athletic condition?
It helps to be in shape. But it's great that people not in shape give it a try. They may fall more than someone in better condition, but that doesn't mean that they're not learning and having fun. I see it as their way of *getting* in better shape. Most people I teach are not in great shape and it's not as much an impediment as one might think.

Is there an ideal time to learn?
Sure. Weather is a big factor. You don't want to learn on

ice. Sometimes in the early spring there are days when the snow melts the day before and freezes overnight. The slopes become sheets of ice in the morning. This condition may cause wrist and shoulder injuries when you fall. It's best to try later in the day when the sun has had a chance to soften things up.

Is snowboarding hard to learn? Is it more difficult than skiing?
Initially it is. But later on the learning curve for snowboarding generally exceeds skiing.

How come skiing is easier at first?
With skiing you have two independent legs for support. With snowboarding you have only one point of balance. It's easier to topple. Both feet are bound and it's more difficult to maintain and regain your stance and balance.

Compare the learning curves of skiing and snowboarding.
In the beginning, the learning goes much faster on skis. I can get a beginner on skis to make turns in an hour. It takes the same beginner three hours to make a simple turn on a snowboard. That's an average, mind you, with one-on-one coaching.

The learning curve in snowboarding is very low and flat until a rider finds his confidence and balance on the board. Then the curve shoots straight up. In skiing it's easier in the beginning but the curve stays on a more gradual track without a dramatic rise.

A snowboarder can tackle steeper hills sooner than a skier because of sideslipping. Sideslipping helps to minimize the fear of steeper slopes and this helps create confidence.

What also happens is that once a snowboarder is comfortable riding on one point of balance, learning comes easier and faster. At first it's easier to balance and progress on skis but the two independent planing surfaces begin to work against more rapid learning because there are two things wobbling around underneath you versus one. So the one point of balance works against you in the beginning, but for you later on.

How important are lessons?

Lessons are very important. As well as a good instructional book! You'll learn safer, faster and have a lot more fun. I don't know how many times I've seen friends try to teach friends with disastrous results. These beginners have such an awful time they never want to snowboard again.

Which is more dangerous, skiing or snowboarding?

If snowboarding is learned with safety in mind it's not a very dangerous sport. Injuries do happen when riders show off or try jumps before they're ready. Snowboards do not have releaseable bindings as do skis and that has caused injuries. Snowboards are also a little more difficult to control than skis.

Is there still tension between snowboarders and skiers?

Yes, but it's better than it used to be. A lot of skiers are showing interest in snowboarding. Most ski resorts have areas for snowboarders only and that helps to separate the two groups. Most snowboarders are young males, seventeen to twenty-one, who can be rude and fearless. We have to remember if they were on skis they'd be just as rude. So a lot of the friction is a function of age. And as I said earlier, snowboards are harder to control than skis. That tends to annoy skiers, too.

Talk about different snow conditions. How about powder?

Powder is freshly fallen snow and can be an exhilarating experience. It's like nothing else. Like boarding on a cloud. It's really fun. And it's not that difficult to ride in. In fact, it's easier for a snowboarder to ride deep powder than a skier.

What conditions do you usually find?

In California, we only get about ten days of deep powder (eight inches or more). Colorado gets more of the light fluffy powder and gets it more often. However, what you usually find at any resort is packed snow. Artificial or natural snow that's groomed by snocats.

Is soft, slushy snow good for snowboarding?

Yeah. It's kinda like powder. It's soft. The snow gives.

What's corn snow?

It's like little ball bearings. It's fun.

What kind of riding do you like?

I like it all. Carving is a lot of fun. It feels like surfing. It's like dropping in on a glassy wave, making a hard on-the-edge bottom turn and sweeping into a roundhouse cutback over and over all the way down the hill. But I like it all — jumps, halfpipe, racing.

What's so great about snowboarding?

It's more than a super, exhilarating sport. It's something to enjoy on different levels. It's the whole experience. The beautiful white snow, the clean air. There's so many people, even in California, who have never seen snow. There's nothing like fresh snow on a sunny day in the mountains. It's magic.

How about your first day on a snowboard?

That was ten years ago. I was on my own. Crashing and burning. My second trip down the mountain I went off the trail into some mud and got covered from head to toe. Luckily I wasn't in my ski instructor's uniform. But I still had fun.

Any parting advise to the reader?

Read and prepare with this guide, take lessons, play it safe and enjoy the experience. You can't help but learn exponentially!

Chapter Twelve:

Safety

Responsibility Code

There are elements of risk in snowboarding that common sense and personal awareness can help reduce. The following seven points make up the Skier's Responsibility Code. Skiers and snowboarders follow the same rules.

1. Snowboard or ski under control and in such a manner that you can stop or avoid other snowboarders and skiers or objects.

2. When snowboarding or skiing downhill or overtaking another snowboarder or skier, you must avoid the snowboarder or skier below you.

3. You must not stop where you obstruct a trail or are not visible to other snowboarders or skiers.

4. When entering a trail or starting downhill, yield to other snowboarders or skiers.

5. All snowboarders and skiers shall use devices to prevent a runaway snowboard or skis.

6. You shall keep off closed trails or posted areas and observe all posted signs.

7. Know how to use the lifts.

When You're Tired, Stop

...and rest. You'll probably exhaust yourself sooner than you think. Especially your first day. Everything is new, awkward and difficult. You can't concentrate when you're fatigued. So take breaks. For as long as it takes.

Be Aware. All the Time

Where are you on the hill? Where is everyone else? Where are you going?

Be in Shape

Hopefully, you are into something on a regular basis that requires a little muscle, a little movement, some lung power and flexibility. When you're in tune with your body, your reactions are quicker. If your body is in shape, you can take the new strains and bruises in stride. You'll have better concentration and you'll last longer. Stretching before you start is always a good idea. You're going to use muscles you never knew you had.

Take Lessons

If you wing it alone or with a "friend who knows how," you're at risk. By yourself you'll destroy yourself. With a "friend who knows how," you'll simply have a captive (maybe) audience.

Be Patient

It's especially difficult to accept your clumsiness if you're actually good at other sports. It's natural, yet unrealistic, to assume that you can immediately transfer your talents to another athletic endeavor. You won't be shredding on a snowboard on your first day, so don't try. Poke around with the fundamentals on little pokey hills. There will be plenty of time for glory later.

Look Ahead

One of the easiest bad habits to get into is looking down at your board. It's pretty natural to gaze down at the vehicle that you think could break your neck, but don't. You won't hurt yourself if you learn on the gentle slopes. But you could run into a tree if you don't look up. Snowboarding is a sport of lickety-split anticipation and reaction. You can't do it without concentrating on the road ahead.

Good Equipment/Good Fit

Boots must fit well and snug without toes hitting the end. All the laces must be there, and the boots must provide firm support. Exactly the same with bindings. Check for loose screws, buckles, etc.

Falling Down

This is a tough one because the worst falls cannot be anticipated. When you catch an edge, you'll slam down before you know it. Catching an edge refers to the downhill edge of your snowboard catching and digging into the snow. What you can do is work on keeping yourself loose as you run through these various exercises. Tumbles will be less of a shock if muscles aren't tense. Tense muscles will cramp your style anyway.

Fear

It's not natural to slip and slide. It's an uncommon feeling and can be frightening. If you're learning on the proper terrain you won't get hurt if you fall. Stay on the gentler slopes and work within your comfort range.

Courtesy

Snowboarders courteous? The terms aren't necessarily

contradictory. Although there has been concern that they just might be. Being a snowboarder only means you slide upon the snow on one planing device, not two. It doesn't mean you have to be a lout. Or that you should expect a snowboarder to be one. There is no physical reason why snowboarders and skiers cannot share the slopes harmoniously. So it comes down to the golden rule: Treat others as you would have them treat you.

If you take the board off while on a hill, lay it bottom up so it doesn't slide away.

Chapter Thirteen:

Early History: 1963-1993

Snowboarding is a very young sport.

The first verifiable snowboard was built in 1963. Manufacturing of boards and organized competition didn't begin until around 1970. It wasn't until 1982 that the first really big contest was held and covered by the major media. It wasn't until 1986 that the first snowboarding instruction was offered at a ski resort. Although resorts had gradually opened their doors since the '70s, it wasn't until 1989 that these major ski areas opened theirs: Squaw Valley (California), Mammoth Mountain (California), Vail (Colorado), Sun Valley (Idaho) and Snowbird (Utah).

Snowboarding is still largely influenced by the very names that invented it: Tom Sims, Dimitrije Milovich, Jake Burton Carpenter, Chuck Barfoot, Paul Graves. They aren't old men.

Here's a year by year summation of major events through 1993. This timeline is graciously provided by *Transworld Snowboarding Magazine* (founded 1987).

Transworld's Snowboarding Historical Timeline
1929: According to a letter sent to *Transworld Snowboarding Magazine*, M. J. "Jack" Burtchett cuts out a piece of plywood, secures his feet to it with horse reins

and clothesline, and surfs the first winter wave. Although he doesn't have a copy of the board or any record, his claim would make him the first person on a snowboard. Even predating skateboards. Any takers?

1963: Tom Sims makes his first "skiboard" for an eighth grade project in New Jersey.

1965: Sherman Poppen invents the Snurfer for his kids by bolting two skis together. He later organizes competitions for Snurfers at the Pando Ski Area in Rockford, Michigan.

1969: Mike Doyle develops the monoski which is a forerunner to the alternative ski concept.

1970: Inspired by sliding on cafeteria trays in upstate New York, east coast surfer Dimitrije Milovich starts developing snowboards "based on surfboard design with a rudimentary idea of how skis work." Milovich claims that the boards had metal edges, which would be fifteen years prior to when they were first believed to have been used.

1971: Milovich is granted a patent for his snowboard design so that he can sell the idea to ski companies. The patent doesn't expire until 1988. Milovich declines from enforcing the patent with other companies.

1969–1972: Bob Webber spends several years trying to obtain a patent for his early "skiboard" design. The patent is granted in 1972. He later sells the patent to Jake Burton Carpenter on August 17, 1990.

1975: Dimitrije Milovich establishes Winterstick Snowboards in Utah. The metal edges that were featured on his earlier boards are removed. "We didn't need them. We were riding in powder over our heads," Milovich now says. Milovich also develops a swallow-tail board based on the same design in surfboards. One year later he gets a patent on a double-edged design.

• Milovich and Winterstick are written up in the March issue of *Newsweek* and have a two-page photo spread in *Powder*, giving snowboarding early national exposure.

1977: Mike Olsen builds his first snowboard in junior high woodshop. He continues to modify boards and in 1984 starts Gnu Snowboards.

• Jake Burton Carpenter moves to Stratton Mountain, Vermont. He works as a bartender at night and designs the prototypes for what will later be Burton Snowboards during the day. Like Sims, he claims to have been modifying Snurfers since high school.

• Milovich obtains a written confirmation from Petit-Morey and Kendall Insurance (the insurance brokers for America's ski resorts) that snowboards are in fact covered under regular ski liability. This proves that resort acceptance is based on the mountain manager's preference, just as suspected.

• Bob Webber designs the "yellow banana" polyethylene molded bottom, and Tom Sims tacks on the Lonnie Toft skate deck to make the first production "Skiboard" under the Sims name.

1978: Milovich says that by this year he has sold Wintersticks in 11 foreign countries.

• In Santa Barbara, surfer/skater Chuck Barfoot develops a fiberglass prototype snowboard. He and Bob Webber take it out to Utah for a test run. Barfoot later designs boards with Tom Sims.

1979: Although Milovich's designs never sold to ski companies as intended, the Hexel ski company produces a double-edged ski and a swallow-tail ski. This is the first evidence of ski design copying snowboarding design.

• At the annual Snurfer contest held in Michigan, sponsored Snurfer pro Paul Graves puts on a freestyle demo and wows the crowd by doing four sliding 360s, dropping down on one knee for part of the course and dismounting from his board at the finish with a front flip.

At the same event, Jake Burton Carpenter tries to enter on his own equipment. There are protests about his non-Snurfer snowboard design. Paul Graves and others stand up for Jake's right to race and an open division is created which only Jake enters and wins.

• Paul Graves rides a Snurfer in the first TV commercial to feature snowboarding. The LaBatt's Beer spot runs four years in Canada and the northern USA.

1979–80: *Skateboarder* and *Action Now* magazines both print some of the earliest features on the rising sport of snowboarding.

1980: Both Burton and Winterstick Snowboards utilize a

P-Tex base on their prototype boards, introducing ski technology to the industry.

1981: After working on early developments at Sims, Chuck Barfoot leaves to form his own company.

• Modern competitive snowboarding begins with a small contest held in April at Ski Cooper in Leadville, Colorado.

1982: Paul Graves organizes the National Snowboarding Championships at Suicide Six Ski Area in Woodstock, Vermont. A slalom and a downhill event are featured. Racers in the downhill are clocked at speeds in excess of 60 mph.

This is the first time riders nationwide have competed against each other including rivals Tom Sims and Jake Burton Carpenter. Burton team rider Doug Bouton wins first overall.

The contest also features the first amateur division. It's the last time Snurfers and snowboards race together. The contest draws media coverage from *Sports Illustrated*, NBC Today and Good Morning America.

1983: Jake Burton Carpenter organizes the National Snowboarding Championships in the spring at Snow Valley, Vermont. Tom Sims then goes home and holds the inaugural World Snowboarding Championships at Soda Springs Ski Bowl in the Lake Tahoe area. This is the first contest to have a halfpipe event.

• Jeff Grell designs the first highback binding, enabling

boards to be ridden effectively on hardpack. The bindings were first used on Flite Snowboards but later developed for Sims Snowboards. Grell makes the history books but never sees any money from his innovation.

1985: *Skateboarder* covers the World Championships at Soda Springs. This is some of the first magazine exposure for a snowboarding event.

• In January, Mt. Baker hosts the first Mt. Baker Legendary Banked Slalom which becomes a competitive mainstay. Tom Sims wins.

• *Absolutely Radical*, the first magazine exclusively about snowboarding, appears in March. Six months later the name changes to *International Snowboard Magazine.*

• Skater Marty Jiminez writes *Transworld Skateboarding's* first snowboard article in the April issue.

• Metal edges are introduced on the Sims 1500 FE and Burton Performer models. This ends the era of surfing-influenced fin design once and for all. Snowboard design begins to incorporate ski technology.

• Sims Snowboards introduces the first signature model snowboard in its winter line, bearing Terry Kidwell's name. The Kidwell is also the first freestyle board with a rounded tail.

• Mike Olsen's Gnu Snowboards are the first to be marketed as carving boards, upon which turns can be made more precisely with less sliding.

1986: Europeans begin to organize their own regional events, such as the Swiss Championships in St. Moritz.

• The Swiss winner of some of those European races, Jose Fernandes, comes to America with an asymmetrical board, the forerunner to today's 'asym' production models. The board is made by his sponsor, Hooger Booger.

• The World Snowboarding Championships, or the World's, as it has become known, relocates from Soda Springs to Breckenridge, Colorado. The March event draws big money from Swatch and generates the most national interest to date. Fran Richards, Paul Alden, and Dave Alden convince the Breckenridge management that the halfpipe is not a high-speed event.

• Stratton Mountain in Vermont becomes the first resort to offer organized snowboarding instruction.

• Sims Snowboards is licensed by Vision in December.

1986–1987: With a lace-up ski-boot inner bladder, Burton Snowboards produces what will become the standard design for soft-boot snowboarding.

1987: Chuck Barfoot and his company introduces the first twin-tip freestyle shape with an identical nose and tail. The board is designed by Canadians Neil Daffern and Ken and Dave Achenbach.

• Europeans host their own World Championships in

January at Livigno, Italy and St. Moritz, Switzerland. This event is not to be confused with the other World Championships held at Breckenridge, Colorado later the same year.

• The day after the second Breckenridge World's in March, Paul Alden and a collection of riders and manufacturers formed the North American Snowboard Association (NASA). The acronym is later changed to NASBA because NASA is already taken. The association's main goal is to work with the Snowboard European Association (SEA) to create a unified world cup tour.

• A host of early snowboarders, including Dave Alden, pen the first Professional Ski Instructors Association (PSIA) Manual for snowboard instructors.

• *Transworld Snowboarding Magazine* publishes its first issue in the fall.

• In September, Wrigley's Chewing Gum utilizes snowboarding in a national commercial. Craig Kelly, Bert LaMar, Tom Burt and Jim Zellers appear in an aerial romp filmed by Greg Stump.

1987–1988: The first World Cup is held throughout the season with two events in Europe and two in the United States. The circuit also introduces major corporate sponsorship (O'Neill, Suzuki and Swatch) into the competitive arena.

1988: Veteran surf company Ocean Pacific (OP) warms up to snowboarding by developing its own line of winter clothing. Other surf companies soon follow and capitalize on the crossover between the two sports.

• Further action sport involvement comes when surf and skate manufacturer G&S enters the market. By 1990, G&S exits the snowboard market.

• While the two major snowboard manufacturers, Burton and Sims, battle over Craig Kelly in court, he is ordered by a federal judge not to ride any products bearing any logo other than Sims. Kelly then starts riding boards with no logo. The restraining order is later reversed and Kelly signs a long-term deal with Burton.

• Former amateur surf promoter Chuck Allen incorporates the United States Amateur Snowboarding Association (USASA) in July with a $500 donation from *Transworld Snowboarding Magazine*. USASA is the first governing body exclusively for competitive amateur snowboarding.

1989: Earl A. Miller, an engineer and inventor from Utah, produces a releaseable snowboard binding, but the technology has yet to hit the mainstream.

• Just in time for winter, most of the major ski resorts that had previously resisted snowboarding succumb. They include Squaw Valley (California), Mammoth Mountain (California), Vail (Colorado), Sun Valley (Idaho) and Snowbird (Utah).

• OP continues to delve into the snowboarding market by expanding their popular OP Pro of Surfing to include the OP Pro of Snowboarding. The contest is held at June Mountain, California.

• The first National Collegiate Championships are held in December at Stratton Mountain, Vermont. Soon, college teams and clubs sprout throughout the country.

1990: Jake Burton Carpenter buys the patent for the "skiboard" from its designer Bob Webber. The industry fears he will make them pay royalties on all board sales. But Burton never pursues the issue, making the patent a moot point.

• The USASA holds its premiere national championships in February, at Snow Valley, California. The worst snowstorm of the decade hits just before the event and closes all roads to Big Bear. Amateur snowboarders from all over the country are left stranded. A rescue caravan of locals led by USASA president Chuck Allen sneaks the competitors past the police barricades and gets them to the contest on time.

• In June, Breckenridge Ski Corporation announces plans to house the Snowboarding Hall of Fame, with artifacts from the sport's not-so-distant past.

• Santa Cruz Skateboards' owner Rich Novak starts producing a line of snowboards. Other skate companies like H-Street decide to test the waters with their own board and clothing designs.

• Vail Ski Resort tries a new approach by developing an inbounds obstacle area called a "snowboard park." The area is intended to cater to a growing snowboarding market and other resorts quickly follow suit.

1991: By now, the pro surfer/pro skater crossover to

snowboarding is prevalent. Skaters Steve Caballero and Lance Mountain have been riding since the early '80s. Tony Hawk, Kevin Staab and Joe Johnson have been riding for years. Recent convert Mike Youssefpour puts in slope time as well. Surf standouts like Gary Elkerton and Noah Budroe bite the snowboarding bait, and most other pro surfers ride regularly, or have tried it.

• After a lengthy court dispute over the Sims name, Tom Sims wins back the licensing rights from Vision in February. Vision begins production under its own name and Sims resumes making a new Sims line.

• The OP Wintersurf contest held in February pits pro surfers and snowboarders against each other in a surf contest at Huntington Beach and a snowboard obstacle course/race at Bear Mountain. Top international pro surfer Gary Elkerton scores the win, proving it's a lot harder to learn how to surf than snowboard.

1993: The International Snowboard Federation holds its first official Snowboard World Championships in Ischgl, Austria. Kevin Delaney and Michele Taggart win the combined titles.

Glossary

Air: The space between board and snow achieved by leaping, jumping, etc.

Alpine: Refers to a type of downhill snowboarding involving high speed and carving turns. Alpine boards are built stiff in order to hold an edge.

Artificial Snow: The snow made by machines at ski areas in order to extend the skiing\snowboarding season.

Asymmetrical: Refers to a snowboard design that is asymmetrical in shape. The angle of the 'asym' is determined by the position of the rider's feet on the board.

Basic Turn: Refers to a directional change that requires a transfer from one edge to the other. A combination of rotation, pressuring and edging techniques effect this turn. Sometimes called a skidded turn.

Barney: A person with all the social skills of Barney Fife, Deputy Sheriff.

Board Corrals: Guarded areas at a ski area where one can stow a snowboard in order to dash into the lodge.

Bonking: Hitting something while riding a snowboard.

Buttplant: Falling on one's butt.

Camber: The bend built into a snowboard. Camber, along with flex and the sidecut, influence the turning capabilities of a board.

Carpet Riding: Snowboard practice on the carpet at home.

Carved Turn: A turn that utilizes a snowboard's edge only. No skidding.

Catching an Edge: Digging the downhill edge of a snowboard into the snow while descending a slope. Usually results in a head- or buttplant.

Counter-intuitive: What does *not* come natural, like heading downhill on a snowboard.

Diagonal Sideslip: A sideslip directed in a particular direction by leaning and shifting weight in that direction.

Edges: The steel strips located along the sides of a snowboard.
Edging: The act of tilting a board on its uphill edge.

Fakie: Riding a snowboard backward.
Fall Line: The path of least resistance down a given slope. The path a ball would take.
Falling Leaf: A beginning riding technique made up of alternating left and right directional sideslips.
Flex: The bendability of a snowboard. Flex affects the turning capability of a snowboard.
Freeride: Refers to an all-around riding style that seeks a balance between freestyle and alpine snowboarding. In theory, freeride boards are loose enough to do freestyle tricks, yet stiff enough to hold a high speed carve.
Freestyle: Refers to snowboarding activity that involves quick turns and trick maneuvers (jumps, halfpipe and terrain garden). Freestyle boards are generally twin-tipped and less stiff, or easy to turn.

Garlands: A traversing technique that entails a series of partial turns across the fall line without an edge change. The track looks like the drooping garland around a Christmas tree, hence the name.
Goofy Foot: Riding a snowboard with the right foot forward.
Grooming: Preparing the snow at a ski area with snow-

cats. Usually a nighttime activity, snocats press down snow, break up ice and fill in dips.

Halfpipe: A walled, U-shaped trough created on a slope on which snowboarders perform aerial maneuvers off its sides.

Hardpack: A snow condition where old snow has settled into a hard mass. Not an ideal surface to ride.

Hard Boot: A snowboarding boot made of hard plastic and worn with plate bindings. Provides maximum support and leverage for high speed carving and racing.

Headplant: Falling on your head.

Heel-side: That side of your snowboard next to your your heels.

Highback Bindings: A type of binding used for freestyle or freeride snowboarding. Used with soft boots. The "high" backs provide necessary ankle support and leverage. Also called freestyle bindings.

Ice: A snow condition where the slope has frozen into a hard sheet. A very difficult surface to snowboard on.

Leash: The strap that attaches the snowboard to the leg.

Lift: The chairlift at a ski area.

Linked Turns: Connected toe- and heel-side turns.

Moguls: The "bumps" made by the tracks of skiers and snowboarders over a period of time on the face of a slope.

Monoski: The single ski concept developed by Mike Doyle in 1969.

Muscle Memory: The body's ability to remember athletic action after training.

Plate Binding: A type of snowboarding binding used for racing or alpine riding with hard boots.

Powder: Usually a freshly fallen snow condition with relatively little moisture content. Riders tend to sink or settle in powder as they ride, requiring specific riding technique. A difficult yet deeply satisfying surface for intermediate and expert riders.

Pressuring: The exerted force of board against snow.

Racing: Downhill snowboarding involving maximum speed and carving turns. A step up from alpine snowboarding in these categories. Racing snowboards are the thinnest and "stiffest" of all snowboards.

Regular Foot: Riding a snowboard with the left foot forward.

Rotation: The body movement that helps to initiate a basic turn.

Shred: To ride a snowboard very, very well.

Sidecut: The concave curve built into the side of a snowboard. A sidecut enhances the turning ability of a snowboard.

Sideslip: To travel down a slope sideways. The length of the board is at right angles to the fall line.

Skating: The act of pushing oneself along on a snowboard with an unbound foot.

Skiboard: The name or label applied to early snowboards developed by Tom Sims and Bob Webber, among others.

Skidded Turn: A basic turn produced by applying specific rotation, pressuring and edging techniques. The bottom of the board skids through a portion of this turn, hence the name.

Slalom: A downhill race where snowboarders or skiers

turn around staggered flags or poles.

Slush: A snow condition where the sun has melted the slopes to a slurpy-like consistency.

Snowboard Park: An area set aside at ski areas for special snowboarding activity. Usually includes a halfpipe and various "playground furniture" to bonk and jump over.

Snocats: The big grooming machines at ski areas. Their tank-like treads mash down snow into a suitable surface for skiing and snowboarding.

Snurfer: The forerunner of the snowboard. Invented in 1965 by Sherman Poppen. The Snurfer was more or less a wide, wooden ski with a rope handle attached to the nose.

Soft Boot: A flexible snowboarding boot designed for freestyle riding.

Step-in Binding: Binding with part of the binding device built into the sole of the snowboard boot. This allows a rider to simply step into the locking device without straps and buckles.

Stomp Pad: The pad between bindings on a snowboard. Here a rider can rest his or her unbound foot while gliding or skating.

Swallow Tail: An early snowboard tail design lifted from surfboard design. Tail is shaped into two points.

360: Spinning or turning 360 degrees on the snow or in the air.

Tail: The rear end of your snowboard.

Tip: The front end of your snowboard.

Toe-side: That side of your snowboard next to your toes.

Transferring Edges: Turning. Refers to the act of shifting the downhill edge of a snowboard to an uphill edge while changing direction.

Traverse: To angle sideways across the face of a slope and the fall line.

Twin-tip: A snowboard with both an up-turned nose and tail enabling the rider to ride forwards or backwards. Associated with freestyle riding.

Unweighting: The act of straightening the legs and lifting in order to "unweight" the board.

Weighting: The act of flexing the knees and allowing a rider's weight to apply pressure to the snowboard.

Wicking: The ability of a garment to draw moisture through itself to outer garments and the open air. A characteristic of well designed outdoor underwear and liner socks.

Resources

Snowboard/Ski/Surf Shops
The best source for information, gear, etc. is a snowboard shop, which can often be found combined with a ski and/or surf shop depending on your locale. Shops should be able to provide you with the best local information about:

- Snowboarding areas
- Snowboarding camps
- Snowboarding schools/lessons
- Snow conditions
- Snowboarding contests
- Snowboarding organizations

Shops also provide:
- Snowboards
- Snowboarding gear
- Snowboarders to talk to
- Snowboarding magazines and literature

Snowboard/ski shops are littered around ski areas, of course, and can be found in major cities within a half-day's drive to the mountains. Beach cities may have combined surf and snowboard shops. Check the yellow pages.

Television
Watch the Prime Ticket Cable Network, ESPN, ESPN2 and MTV for occasional snowboarding programs. They aren't prolific but they're there sometimes. Also the ISF (International Snowboard Federation) Media Network has channel access in 67 countries. Check listings.

Videos
There are a lot of videos showing the very best riders doing the impossible. Find them at shops and stores next to or around ski areas. Blockbuster is a good bet.

Transworld Snowboarding has the best instructional video to date. 619-722-7777

Snowboarding Organizations
International Snowboard Federation (ISF)
PO Box 5688
Snowmass Village, Colorado 81615
970-923-7669
www.isfna.com

United States Amateur Snowboarding Association
(USASA)
315 East Alcott Avenue
Fergus Falls, MN 56537
www.usasa.org

U.S. Snowboarding
PO Box 100
Park City, UT 84060
801-649-9090

American Association of Snowboard Instructors (AASI)
133 South Van Gordon Street
Suite 101
Lakewood, CO 80228
303-987-9390
www.psia.org

Canadian Snowboard Federation
2440 Place Prevel, Apt. #8
Sainte-Foy, Quebec G1V 2X3
418-688-9781

Ski Industries of America (SIA)
8377-B Greensboro Drive
McLean, VA 22102
703-821-8276

Books
The Complete Snowboarder
By Jeff Bennett
Ragged Mountain Press, 1994

The Snowboard Book
By Lowell Hart
W.W. Norton, 1997

Snowboarding Know-How
By Cristof Weiss
Sterling Publishing, 1993

Magazines
Backcountry
7065 Dover Way
Arvada, CO 80004
303-424-5858

Powder
PO Box 1028
Dana Point, CA 92629

Skiing
2 Park Avenue
New York, NY 10016
212-779-5000

Snow Country
5520 Park Avenue
Trumbull, CT 06611
203-373-7000

Snowboard Canada
2255 B Queen Street E
Suite 3266
Toronto, Ontario
Canada M4E 1G3
416-698-0138

Snowboard Life
353 Airport Road
Oceanside, CA 92054
619-722-7777

Snowboarder
33046 Calle Aviador
San Juan Capistrano, CA 92675
714-496-5922

Transworld Snowboarding
353 Airport Road
Oceanside, CA 92054
619-722-7777

Bibliography

Bennett, Jeff. The Complete Snowboarder. Camden, Maine: Ragged Mountain Press, 1994.

Berry, I. William. The Great American Ski Book. New York, New York: Charles Scribner's Sons, 1982.

Campbell, Stu. The Way to Ski! Tucson, Arizona: The Body Press, 1986.

Fodor's Skiing in North America. New York, New York: Fodor's Travel Publications, Inc., 1989.

Gamma, Carl. The Handbook of Skiing. New York, New York: Alfred A. Knopf, Inc., 1989.

Hart, Lowell. The Snowboard Book. New York, New York: W. W Norton, 1997.

Masia, Seth. Ski Magazine's Managing the Mountain. New York, New York: Simon and Schuster, 1992.

Professional Ski Instructors of America. Snowboard Skiing. 1993.

Professional Ski Instructors of America. Snowboard Certification Training Manual. 1997.

Snowboarder Magazine. San Juan Capistrano, California: Surfer Publications, Inc.

Transworld Snowboarding Magazine. Oceanside, California: Transworld Media.

Index

Alpine boards 32-33

Basic moves on snow 53-59
Basic turn 91-96
Binding angles 34, 35, 36
Bindings 33-34
Board corrals 50
Boots 31-32

Camber 19
Carpet riding, basic moves 39-44
Carving 100-102
Climbing up a hill on a snowboard 59

Diagonal sideslipping 62, 63, 64, 82, 83

Edges 18, 55, 87, 88

Fall line 20
Falling 53, 66, 67, 69-70
Falling leaf 80, 81, 82
Fear 22
Flex 18
Form 90, 99
Freeride boards 33
Freestyle bindings 33
Freestyle boards 32

Garlands 84, 85, 86
Gear 26-29

Hard boot settings 35, 36

Heel-side turn 94
History 115-125

Leash 19
Lifts 73-77
Linked turns 97

Physical considerations 23-24
Physics 20
Plate bindings 34
Preparations 45-49
Pressuring 20, 21

Ready position 36, 54
Rotation 20, 21, 42-43, 57

Safety 111-114
Sidecut 18,19
Sideslipping 62, 63, 80, 87
Signs 50-51
Skateboarding 14-15
Skating 58
Skiers versus snowboarders, conflict 11
Skiing 14
Sliding 60-61
Snowboard anatomy 17-19
Snowboarding, growth statistics 9
Snowboards 32-33
Soft boot settings 35
Stance, which foot forward 36
Step-in bindings 34
Stomp pad 19
Stopping 64, 65, 66
Surfing 13-14

Toe brake 60-61
Toe-side turn 93
Traversing 20
Turns 20, 91-102
Turning formula 92

Waide, Jim 139
Waide, Jim interview 103-110
Walking the snowboard 40-41, 56

About the Author & Start-Up Sports

Doug Werner is the author of all ten books in the *Start-Up Sports Series* including *Surfer's, Snowboarder's, Sailor's, In-Line Skater's, Bowler's, Longboarder's, Golfer's, Fencer's, Boxer's and Backpacker's Start-Up*. He has been interviewed on CNN and numerous radio talk shows throughout the United States. His books have appeared on ESPN, been featured in prominent national publications, and sold throughout the United States, Canada, Great Britain and Japan.

The series celebrates the challenge of learning a new sport with emphasis on basic technique, safety and fun. Imbued with a unique beginner's perspective, *Start-Up* books explain and explore what it's really like to learn.

Each book has the endorsement of prominent individuals, publications and organizations in each respective sport including Steve Hawk of *Surfer Magazine*, Ted Martin of International Snowboard Federation, Chuck Nichols of America's Cup 1995, *Bowler's Journal, Longboarder Magazine, Ski Magazine, Snow Country, Veteran Fencer's Quarterly* and many others.

The series has received critical acclaim from *Booklist, Library Journal, Outside Kids, Boys Life, The San Francisco Examiner* and *The Orange County Register.*

Werner is a graduate of Cal State Long Beach and holds a degree in fine arts. In previous lifetimes he established a graphics business in 1980, an advertising agency in 1984 and yet another graphics business in 1987. By 1993 he had decided to move on and began writing sport instructional guides. In 1994 he established Tracks Publishing and the *Start-Up Sports* series. Doug has pursued a sporting lifestyle his entire life and has resided in San Diego, California, one of the planet's major sport funzones, since 1980.

142

About Co-Author Jim Waide

Jim Waide is one of the nation's leading snowboard and ski instructors. For four straight years he's been chosen as one of Skiing Magazine's Top 100 Instructors in the United States. As an official examiner with the American Association of Snowboard Instructors (AASI) he certifies other instructors in clinics and tests throughout California.

Waide has instructed and has been a consultant at Mammoth and Snow Summit Ski Resorts. He has been featured in numerous mountain sport publications and advises the AASI on its training manuals.

After 25 years on the hill and nearly a decade of teaching experience, Jim has successfully introduced thousands of all ages to the thrills of snowboarding and skiing.

In the '70s Jim was one of the premier shapers of surfboards in Southern California. He has designed and shaped over 8,000 surfboards. Of course, these days Jim designs and produces snowboards as well.

Jim lives and works out of Big Bear Lake, California.

Jim Waide
PO Box 774
Big Bear Lake, CA 92315
E-Mail: insports@gte.net
ICQ# 13766251

Ordering More Start-Up Sports Books:

The Start-Up Sports series:

- ❏ Surfer's Start-Up
- ❏ Snowboarder's Start-Up
- ❏ Sailor's Start-Up
- ❏ In-line Skater's Start-Up
- ❏ Bowler's Start-Up
- ❏ Longboarder's Start-Up
- ❏ Golfer's Start-Up
- ❏ Fencer's Start-Up
- ❏ Boxer's Start-Up
- ❏ Backpacker's Start-Up

Each book costs $12.95 (includes priority postage) Send a check for this amount to:

Tracks Publishing
140 Brightwood Avenue
Chula Vista, CA 91910

Or call 1-800-443-3570.
Visa and MasterCard accepted.

Start-Up Sports books are available in all major bookstores and selected sporting goods stores.

www.startupsports.com

Start-UpSports®
celebrating the challenge